Decision-Making For Managers

The Jataka Way

Luis S. R. Vas
Anita S. R. Vas

UNICORN BOOKS

Publishers
UNICORN BOOKS
F-2/16, Ansari Road, Daryaganj, New Delhi-110002
☎ 23275434, 23262683, 23262783 • Fax: 011-23257790
E-mail: info@unicornbooks.in • *Website:* www.unicornbooks.in

Distributors
Pustak Mahal®
J-3/16, Daryaganj, New Delhi-110002
☎ 23276539, 23272783, 23272784 • Fax: 011-23260518
E-mail: info@pustakmahal.com • *Website:* www.pustakmahal.com

Sales Centres
- 10-B, Netaji Subhash Marg, Daryaganj, New Delhi-110002
  ☎ 23268292, 23268293, 23279900 • Fax: 011-23280567
  E-mail: salespmahal@airtelmail.in, rapidexdelhi@indiatimes.com
- 6686, Khari Baoli, Delhi-110006
  ☎ 23944314, 23911979
- **Bengaluru:** ☎ 080-22234025 • Telefax: 080-22240209
  E-mail: pustak@airtelmail.in • pustak@sancharnet.in
- **Mumbai:** ☎ 022-22010941, 022-22053387
  E-mail: rapidex@bom5.vsnl.net.in
- **Patna:** ☎ 0612-3294193 • Telefax: 0612-2302719
  E-mail: rapidexptn@rediffmail.com
- **Hyderabad:** Telefax: 040-24737290
  E-mail: pustakmahalhyd@yahoo.co.in

ISBN 978-81-7806-193-1

Edition: April, 2010

Printed at : Param Offsetters, Okhla, New Delhi-110020

Contents

Introduction

Jataka is the technical name, in Buddhist literature, for a story of one or other of the previous births of the Buddha, in the Buddhist canon. This is the most ancient and the most complete collection of folklore now extant in any literature in the world. Since it was made around the 3rd century B.C., it can be trusted not to give any of that modern or European colouring which renders suspect much of the folklore collected by modern travellers.

In adopting the folklore and fables already current in India, the Buddhists did not change them very much. The stories as preserved for us, are for the most part Indian rather than Buddhist.

The Jataka stories, over millennia, have been seminal for the development of many civilisations, the cultivation of moral conduct and good behaviour, the growth of a rich and varied literature in diverse parts of the world and the inspiration for painting, sculpture and architecture of enduring aesthetic value. The Buddha himself used Jataka stories to explain concepts like *kamma* (caste) and rebirth and to emphasise the importance of certain moral values.

In India, these and similar other stories were instrumental in the socialisation of children, discouraging them from selfishness and laying foundations for family and community solidarity. Jataka stories speak eloquently of those human values which contribute to harmony, pleasure, progress and ultimately to happiness.

These stories are more relevant in the fragmented societies of today, where especially children and youth, in their most formative years, seek helplessly for guidance in steering their lives to success and fulfilment through correct decision-making.

They have also been used in corporate management workshops on decision-making based on traditional Indian values which tend to be forgotten in today's cut-throat competition.

We have collected some of the Jataka tales and appended to each of them insights for enlightened decision-making. We conclude the book with a chapter which will help you tie up your newly discovered decision-making insights to modern management techniques so that your decisions make the best of both worlds.

Luis S. R. Vas
Anita S. R. Vas
luissrvas@gmail.com

1

Crossing the Wilderness

While the Master was staying at Jetavana monastery near Savatthi, the wealthy banker, Anathapindika, went one day to pay his respects. His servants carried lots of flowers, perfume, butter, oil, honey, molasses, cloths, and robes. Anathapindika paid obeisance to the Master, presented the offerings he had brought, and sat down respectfully. At that time, Anathapindika was accompanied by five hundred friends who were followers of heretical teachers. His friends also paid their respects to the Master and sat close to the banker. The Master's face appeared like a full moon, and his body was surrounded by a radiant aura. Seated on the red stone seat, he was like a young lion roaring with a clear, noble voice as he taught them a discourse full of sweetness and musical to the ear.

After hearing the Master's teaching, the five hundred gave up their heretical practices and took refuge in the Triple Gem: the Buddha, the *Dhamma* (Dharma or truth), and the Sangha. After that, they went regularly with Anathapindika to offer flowers and incense and to hear the teaching. They gave liberally, kept the precepts, and faithfully observed the Uposatha Day. Soon after the Master left Savatthi to return to Rajagaha, however, these men abandoned their new faith and reverted to their previous beliefs.

Seven or eight months later, the Master returned to Jetavana. Again, Anathapindika brought these friends to visit the Buddha. They paid their respects, but Anathapindika explained that they had forsaken their refuge and had resumed their original practices.

The Master asked, "Is it true that you have abandoned refuge in the Triple Gem for refuge in other doctrines?" The Master's voice was incredibly clear because throughout myriad aeons he had always spoken truthfully.

When these men heard it, they were unable to conceal the truth. "Yes, Blessed One," they confessed. "It is true."

"Disciples," the Master said "nowhere between the lowest of hells below and the highest heaven above, nowhere in all the infinite worlds that stretch right and left, is there the equal, much less the superior, of a Buddha. Incalculable is the excellence which springs from obeying the Precepts and from other virtuous conduct."

Then he declared the virtues of the Triple Gem. "By taking refuge in the Triple Gem," he told them, "one escapes from rebirth in states of suffering." He further explained that meditation on the Triple Gem leads through the four stages to Enlightenment.

"In forsaking such a refuge as this," he admonished them, "you have certainly erred. In the past, too, men who foolishly mistook what was no refuge for a real refuge, met disaster. Actually, they fell prey to *yakkhas* -- evil spirits -- in the wilderness and were utterly destroyed. In contrast, men who clung to the truth not only survived, but actually prospered in that same wilderness."

Anathapindika raised his clasped hands to his forehead, praised the Buddha, and asked him to tell that story of the past.

"In order to dispel the world's ignorance and to conquer suffering," the Buddha proclaimed, "I practised the Ten Perfections for countless aeons. Listen carefully, and I will speak."

Having their full attention, the Master made clear, as though he were releasing the full moon from behind the clouds, what rebirth had concealed from them.

Long, long ago, when Brahmadatta was reigning in Varanasi, the Master was born into a merchant's family and grew up to be a wise trader. At the same time, in the same city, there was another merchant, a very stupid fellow, with no common sense whatsoever.

One day it so happened that the two merchants each loaded five hundred carts with costly wares of Varanasi and prepared to leave in the same direction and at exactly the same time. The wise merchant thought, "If this silly young fool travels with me and if our thousand carts stay together, it will be too much for the road. Finding wood and water for the men will be difficult, and there won't be enough grass for the oxen. Either he or I must go first."

"Look," he said to the other merchant, "the two of us can't travel together. Would you rather go first or follow after me?"

The foolish trader thought, "There will be many advantages if I take the lead. I'll get a road which is not yet cut up. My oxen will have the pick of the grass. My men will get the choicest wild herbs for curry. The water will be undisturbed. Best of all, I'll be able to fix my own price for bartering my goods." Considering all these advantages, he said, "I will go ahead of you, my friend."

The Master was pleased to hear this because he saw many advantages in following after. He reasoned, "Those carts going first will level the road where it is rough, and I'll be able to travel along the road they have already smoothed. Their oxen will graze off the coarse old grass, and mine will pasture on the sweet young growth which will spring up in its place. My men will find fresh sweet herbs for curry where the old ones have been picked. Where there is no water, the first caravan will have to dig to supply themselves, and we'll be able to drink at the wells they have dug. Haggling over prices is tiring work; he'll do the work, and I will be able to barter my wares at prices he has already fixed."

"Very well, my friend," he said, "please go first."

"I will," said the foolish merchant, and he yoked his carts and set out. After a while he came to the outskirts of a wilderness. He filled all his huge water jars with water before setting out to cross the desert which lay before him.

The *yakkha* who haunted that wilderness had been watching the caravan. When it had reached the middle, he used his magic power to conjure up a lovely carriage drawn by pure white young bulls. With a retinue of a dozen disguised *yakkha*s carrying swords and shields, he rode along in his carriage like a mighty Lord. His hair and clothes were wet, and he had a wreath of blue lotuses and white water lilies around his head. His attendants also were dripping wet and draped in garlands. Even the bulls' hooves and carriage wheels were muddy.

As the wind was blowing from the front, the merchant was riding at the head of his caravan to escape the dust. The *yakkha* drew his carriage beside the merchant's and greeted him kindly. The merchant returned the greeting and moved his own carriage to one side to allow the carts to pass while he and the *yakkha* chatted.

"We are on our way from Varanasi, sir," explained the merchant. "I see that your men are all wet and muddy and that you have lotuses and water lilies. Did it rain while you were on the road? Did you come across pools with lotuses and water lilies?"

"What do you mean?" the *yakkha* exclaimed. "Over there is the dark-green streak of a jungle. Beyond that there is plenty of water. It is always raining there, and there are many lakes with lotuses and water lilies." Then, pretending to be interested in the merchant's business, he asked, "What do you have in these carts?"

"Expensive merchandise," answered the merchant.

"What is in this cart which seems so heavily laden?" the *yakkha* asked as the last cart rolled by.

"That's full of water."

"You were wise to carry water with you this far, but there is no need for it now, since water is so abundant ahead. You could travel much faster and lighter without those heavy jars. You'd be better off breaking them and throwing the water away. Well, good day," he said suddenly, as he turned his carriage. "We must be on our way. We have stopped too long already." He rode away quickly with his men. As soon as they were out of sight, he turned and made his way back to his own city.

The merchant was so foolish that he followed the *yakkha's* advice. He broke all the jars, without saving even a single cupful of water, and ordered the men to drive on quickly. Of course, they did not find any water, and they were soon exhausted from thirst. At sunset they drew their carts into a circle and tethered the oxen to the wheels, but there was no water for the weary animals. Without water, the men could not cook any rice either. They sank to the ground and fell asleep. As soon as night came, the *yakkhas* attacked, killing every single man and beast. The fiends devoured the flesh, leaving only the bones, and departed. Skeletons were strewn in every direction, but the five hundred carts stood with their loads untouched. Thus the heedless young merchant was the sole cause of the destruction of the entire caravan.

Allowing six weeks to pass after the foolish trader had left, the Bodhisatta set out with his five hundred carts. When he reached the edge of the wilderness, he filled his water jars. Then he assembled his men and announced, "Let not so much as a handful of water be used without my permission. Furthermore, there are poisonous plants in this wilderness. Do not eat any leaf, flower, or fruit which you have never eaten before, without showing it to me first." Having thus carefully warned his men, he led the caravan into the wilderness.

When they had reached the middle of the wilderness, the *yakkha* appeared on the path just as before. The merchant noticed his red eyes and fearless manner and suspected something strange. "I know there is no water in this desert," he said to himself.

"Furthermore, this stranger casts no shadow. He must be a *yakkha*. He probably tricked the foolish merchant, but he doesn't realise how clever I am."

"Get out of here!" he shouted at the *yakkha*. "We are men of business. We do not throw away our water before we see where more is to come from!"

Without saying any more, the *yakkha* rode away.

As soon as the *yakkhas* had left, the merchant's men approached their leader and said, "Sir, those men were wearing lotuses and water lilies on their heads. Their clothes and hair were wringing wet. They told us that up ahead there is a thick forest where it is always raining. Let us throw away our water so that we can proceed quicker with lightened carts."

The merchant ordered a halt and summoned all his men. "Has any man among you ever heard before today," he asked, "that there was a lake or a pool in this wilderness?"

"No, sir," they answered. "It's known as the 'Waterless Desert.'"

"We have just been told by some strangers that it is raining in the forest just ahead. How far does a rain-wind carry?"

"A *yojana* (equal to about seven miles), sir."

"Has any man here seen the top of even a single storm-cloud?"

"No, sir."

"How far off can you see a flash of lightning?"

"Four or five *yojanas*, sir."

"Has any man here seen a flash of lightning?"

"No, sir."

"How far off can a man hear a peal of thunder?"

"Two or three *yojanas*, sir."

"Has any man here heard a peal of thunder?"

"No, sir."

"Those were not men, but *yakkhas*," the wise merchant told his men.

"They are hoping that we will throw away our water. Then, when we are weak and faint, they will return to devour us. Since the young merchant who went before us was not a man of good sense, most likely he was fooled by them. We may expect to find his carts standing just as they were first loaded. We will probably see them today. Press on with all possible speed, without throwing away a drop of water!"

Just as the merchant had predicted, his caravan soon came upon the five hundred carts with the skeletons of men and oxen strewn in every direction. He ordered his men to arrange his carts in a fortified circle, to take care of the oxen, and to prepare an early supper for themselves. After the animals and men had all safely bedded down, the merchant and his foremen, swords in hand, stood guard all through the night.

At daybreak the merchant replaced his own weak carts for stronger ones and exchanged his own common goods for the most costly of the abandoned merchandise. When he arrived at his destination, he was able to barter his stock of wares at two or three times their value. He returned to his own city without losing a single man out of all his company.

This story ended, the Master said, "Thus it was, laymen, that in times past, the foolish came to utter destruction, while those who clung to the truth escaped from the *yakkhas*' hands, reached their goal in safety, and returned to their homes again.

"This clinging to the truth not only endows happiness even up to rebirth in the Realm of Brahma, but also leads ultimately to Arahatship. Following untruth entails rebirth either in the four states of punishment or in the lowest conditions of mankind." After the Master had expounded the Four Truths, those five hundred disciples were established in the Fruit of the First Path.

The Master concluded his lesson as follows: "The foolish young merchant was Devadatta, and his men were Devadatta's followers. The wise merchant's men were the followers of the Buddha, and I myself was that wise merchant."

Insight: *Don't base your decisions on first impressions. They can be very misleading. Learn to observe and think before jumping to wrong conclusions. Look at all the evidence before reasoning from it, and don't hesitate to ask for all the facts you need before reaching your decision.*

If you get your data from a stranger at least you need to know that this new contact is reliable. If you know nothing about their credentials, it is obviously risky to rely on the data and a matter of common sense to try to check out the facts yourself especially if they are important enough for your survival to depend on them.

2

A Good Friend

The Master told this story at Jetavana monastery about a pious layfollower. One evening, when this faithful disciple came to the bank of the Aciravati river on his way to Jetavana to hear the Buddha, there was no boat at the landing stage. The ferrymen had pulled their boats onto the far shore and had gone themselves to hear the Buddha. The disciple's mind was so full of delightful thoughts of the Buddha, however, that even though he walked into the river, his feet did not sink below the surface and he walked across the water as if he were on dry land. When, however, he noticed the waves on reaching the middle of the river, his ecstasy subsided and his feet began to sink. But as soon as he again focused his mind on the qualities of the Master, his feet rose and he was able to continue walking joyously over the water. When he arrived at Jetavana, he paid his respects to the Master and took a seat on one side.

"Good layman," the Master said, addressing the disciple, "I hope you had no mishap on your way."

"Venerable sir," the disciple replied, "while coming here, I was so absorbed in thoughts of the Buddha that, when I came to the river, I was able to walk across it as though it were solid."

"My friend," the Master said, "you're not the only one who has been protected in this way. In olden days pious laymen were shipwrecked in mid-ocean and saved themselves by remembering the virtues of the Buddha." At the man's request, the Master told this story of the past.

Long, long ago, at the time of the Buddha Kassapa, a lay disciple who had already entered the path booked passage on a ship along with one of his friends, a rich barber. The barber's wife asked this disciple to look after her husband.

A week after the ship left the port, it sank in mid-ocean. The two friends saved themselves by clinging to a plank and were at last cast up on a deserted island. Famished, the barber killed some birds, cooked them, and offered a share of his meal to the follower of the Buddha.

"No, thank you," he answered, "I am fine." Then he thought to himself, "In this isolated place, there is no help for us except the Triple Gem." As he sat meditating on the Triple Gem, a Naga king who had been born on that island transformed himself into a beautiful ship filled with the seven precious things. The three masts were made of sapphire, the planks and anchor of gold, and the ropes of silver.

The helmsman, who was a spirit of the sea, stood on the deck and cried, "Any passengers for India?"

"Yes," the lay disciple answered, "that's where we are bound."

"Then come on board," the sea spirit said.

The layman climbed aboard the beautiful ship and turned to call his friend the barber.

"You may come," the sea spirit said, "but he may not."

"Why not?" the disciple asked.

"He is not a follower of the holy life," answered the sea spirit.

"I brought this ship for you, but not for him."

"In that case," the layman announced, "all the gifts I have given, all the virtues I have practised, all the powers I have developed -- I give the fruit of all of them to him!"

"Thank you, Master!" cried the barber.

"Very well," said the sea spirit, "now I can take you both aboard."

The ship carried the two men over the sea and up the Ganges river. After depositing them safely at their home in Varanasi, the sea spirit used his magic power to create enormous wealth for both of them. Then, poising himself in mid-air, he instructed the men and their friends, "Keep company with the wise and good," he said. "If this barber had not been in company with this pious layman, he would have perished in the middle of the ocean." Finally, the sea spirit returned to his own abode, taking the Naga king with him.

Having finished this discourse, the Buddha taught the *Dhamma*, after which the pious layman entered on the fruit of the second path. "On that occasion," the Buddha said, "the disciple attained arahantship. Sariputta was the Naga king, and I myself was the spirit of the sea."

Insight 1: *Listen to precepts of the wise and true friends in your decisions and you will be wise and lucky yourself. Otherwise you will be led astray by those who think they are powerful but whose power is deceptive and short-lived. You too should extend the hand of true friendship so that others benefit from your knowledge, skills and wisdom without thought of reward. Reward will come to you at an appropriate time which is most beneficial to you. If the good of others is paramount in your mind the excellent relationships you will develop with all those around you will be reward enough – and the blessings you will attract to yourself will be a bonus.*

Insight 2: *Acknowledging the existence of God and finding time to engage our mind with godly thoughts can help accomplish the journey of life smoothly – it allows us to remain tranquil and steadfast through hardships and difficult times. In addition, godliness can even attain things that are just short of miracles in our life — we may usually refer to these instances as 'strokes of luck' which are not logically explained. A good relationship with God besides being personally fulfilling and rewarding would even benefit the people who are close to us, who keep us company. So also, it would be to our advantage to make a decision to "keep company with the wise and good," as a matter of principle. We may be preempted from most of the difficult decision-making by more frequent 'strokes of luck'.*

3

A Lesson for Kings

ONCE upon a time, when Brahmadatta was reigning over Varanasi, the Master returned to life as his son and heir. And when the day came for choosing a name, they called him Prince Brahmadatta. He grew up in due course. When he was sixteen years old, he went to Takxasila, and became accomplished in all arts. And after his father died he ascended the throne, and ruled the kingdom with righteousness and equity. He gave judgments without partiality, hatred, ignorance, or fear. Since he thus reigned with justice, his ministers also administered the law with justice. Law-suits being thus decided with justice, there were none who brought false cases. And as these ceased, the noise and tumult of litigation ceased in the king's court. Though the judges sat all day in the court, they had to leave without any one coming for justice. It came to this, that the Hall of Justice would have to be closed!

Then the Master thought, "It cannot be from my reigning with righteousness that none comes for judgment; the bustle has ceased, and the Hall of Justice will have to be closed. I must, therefore, now examine my own faults; and if I find that anything is wrong in me, put that away, and practise only virtue."

Thenceforth he sought someone to tell him his faults, but among those around him he found no one who would tell him of any fault, but heard only his own praise.

Then he thought, "It is from fear of me that these men speak only good things, and not evil things," and he sought among those people who lived outside the palace. And finding no fault-finder there, he sought among those who lived outside the city, in the suburbs, at the four gates. And there too finding no one to find fault, and hearing only his own praise, he determined to search the country places.

So he made over the kingdom to his ministers, and mounted his chariot; and taking only his charioteer, left the city in disguise. And searching the country through, up to the very boundary, he found no fault-finder, and heard only of his own virtue; and so he turned back from the outermost boundary, and returned by the high road towards the city.

Now at that time the King of Kosala, Mallika by name, was also ruling his kingdom with righteousness; and when seeking for some fault in himself, he also found no faultfinder in the palace, but only heard of his own virtue ! So seeking in country places, he too came to that very spot. And these two came face to face in a low cart-track with precipitous sides, where there was no space for a chariot to get out of the way !

Then the charioteer of Mallika the king said to the charioteer of the King of Benares, "Take thy chariot out of the way !"

But he said, "Take thy chariot out of the way, O Charioteer ! In this chariot sitteth the lord over the kingdom of Varanasi, the great king Brahmadatta."

Yet the other replied, "In this chariot, O Charioteer, sitteth the lord over the kingdom of Kosala, the great king Mallika. Take thy carriage out of the way, and make room for the chariot of our king !"

Then the charioteer of the King of Varanasi thought, "They say then that he too is a king ! What *is* now to be done ?" After some consideration, he said to himself, "I know a way. I'll find out how old he is, and then I'll let the chariot of the younger be got out of the way, and so make room for the elder."

And when he had arrived at that conclusion, he asked that charioteer what the age of the King of Kosala was. But on inquiry he found that the ages of both were equal. Then he inquired about the extent of his kingdom, and about his army, and his wealth, and his renown, and about the country he lived in, and his caste and tribe and family. And he found that both were lords of a kingdom three hundred leagues in extent; and that in respect of army and wealth and renown, and the countries in which they lived, and their caste and their tribe and their family, they were just on a par !

Then he thought, "I will make way for the most righteous." And he asked, "What kind of righteousness has this king of yours."

Then the charioteer of the King of Kosala, proclaiming his king's wickedness as goodness, uttered the First Stanza:

"The strong he overthrows by strength, The mild by mildness, does Mallika; the good he conquers by goodness, and the wicked by wickedness too. Such is the nature of this king! Move out of the way, O Charioteer "

But the charioteer of the King of Varanasi asked him, "Well, have you told all the virtues of your king?"

"Yes," said the other.

"If these are his *virtues,* where are then his faults ?" replied he.

The other said, "Well, for the nonce they shall be faults, if you like! But pray, then, what is the kind of goodness your king has ?"

And then the charioteer of the King of Varanasi called unto him to hearken, and uttered the Second Stanza:

"Anger he conquers by calmness, And by goodness the wicked; The stingy he conquers by gifts, And by truth the speaker of lies. Such is the nature of *this* king! 'Move out of the way, O Charioteer !"

And when he had thus spoken, both Mallika the king and his charioteer alighted from their chariot. And they took out the horses, and removed their chariot, and made way for the King of Varanasi.

Insight: *In the long run calm, goodness, generosity and truth triumph over anger, wickedness and lies. It is important to take your decisions when you have your emotions under control.*

The King of Varanasi earned the respect of another king and fellow traveller based on his goodness and other qualities like calm, generosity and truth. In the modern day too your reputation travels before you-- there isn't much about our character that we can hide for too long. So working for the development of a straight character can have its rewards to the point of turning your decision-making into an easier task. Like it happened to the King of Varanasi, more often than not, with a similar character, the respect you earn moves obstacles, opens roads for yourself and smoothens your life, rendering decision-making easier.

4

The Lion and the Crane

The Master was at one time born in the region of Himavanta as a white crane; now Brahmadatta was at that time reigning in Varanasi. Now it chanced that as a lion was eating meat, a bone stuck in his throat. The throat became swollen, he could not take food, his suffering was terrible. The crane seeing him, as he was perched on a tree looking for food, asked, "What ails thee, friend?" He told him why. "I could free thee from that bone, friend, but dare not enter thy mouth for fear thou mightest eat me." "Don't be afraid, friend, I'll not eat thee; only save my life." "Very well," says he, and caused him to lie down on his left side. But thinking to himself, "Who knows what this fellow will do?" he placed a small stick upright between his two jaws that he could not close his mouth, and inserting his head inside his mouth struck one end of the bone with his beak. Whereupon the bone dropped and fell out. As soon as he had caused the bone to fall, he got out of the lion's mouth, striking the stick with his beak so that it fell out, and then settled on a branch. The lion got well, and one day was eating a buffalo he had killed. The crane, thinking 'I will sound him," settled on a branch just over him, and in conversation spoke this first verse:

"A service have we done thee to the best of our ability, King of the Beasts! Your Majesty! What return shall we get from thee?"

In reply the Lion spoke the second verse:

"As I feed on blood, and always hunt for prey, 'Tis much that thou art still alive having once been between my teeth."

Then in reply the crane said the two other verses :

"Ungrateful, doing no good, not doing as he would be done by, in him there is no gratitude, to serve him is useless."

"His friendship is not won by the clearest good deed. Better softly withdraw from him, neither envying nor abusing."

And having thus spoken the crane flew away.

Insight: *Gratitude is an infallible index of the strength of your character. If you lack it, you lack an indispensable moral quality which you should immediately redress, in your own interest. Or you run the risk of people avoiding you and your friendship.*

The crane was very clear on two counts 1) if a friend does not feel grateful enough to wish to return a favour to you then his friendship is useless. 2) Despite his ungratefulness if he thinks further that you should be happy because he has never harmed you, then you really need to part ways without bothering to even reprimand him.

5

The Demon with the Matted Hair

When Brahmadatta was King of Varanasi, the Bodhisatta was born as son of his chief queen. On his name-day they asked 800 Brahmans, having satisfied them with all their desires, about his lucky marks. The Brahmans who had skill in divining from such marks beheld the excellence of his, and answered :

"Full of goodness, great King, is your son, and when you die he will become king; he shall be famous and renowned for his skill with the five weapons, and shall be the chief man in all India."

On hearing what the Brahmans had to say, they gave him the name of the Prince of the Five Weapons—sword, spear, bow, battle-axe, and shield.

When he came to years of discretion, and had attained the measure of sixteen years, the King said to him :

"My son, go and complete your education."

"Who shall be my teacher ?" the lad asked.

"Go, my son; in the kingdom of Kandahar, in the city of Takxasila, is a far-famed teacher from whom I wish you to learn. Take this, and give it him for a fee." With that he gave him a thousand pieces of money, and sent him.

The lad departed and was educated by this teacher; he received the Five Weapons from him as a gift, bade him farewell, and leaving Takxasila, he began his journey to Varanasi, armed with the Five Weapons.

On his way he came to a forest inhabited by the Demon with the Matted Hair. On entering the forest some men saw him, and cried out:

"Hullo, young sir, keep clear of that wood ! There's a Demon in it called He of the Matted Hair : he kills every man he sees !" And they tried to stop him. But the Bodhisatta, having confidence in himself, went straight on, fearless as a maned lion.

When he reached mid-forest the Demon showed himself. He made himself as tall as a palm-tree; his head was the size of a pagoda, his eyes as big as saucers, and he had two tusks all over knobs and bulbs ; he had the face of a hawk, a variegated belly, and blue hands and feet.

"Where are you going ?" he shouted. "Stop ! You'll make a meal for me !"

Said the Bodhisatta: "Demon, I came here trusting in myself. I advise you to be careful how you come near me. Here's a poisoned arrow, which I'll shoot at you and knock you down !" With this menace, he fitted to his bow an arrow dipped in deadly poison, and let fly. The arrow stuck fast in the Demon's hair. Then he shot and shot, till he had shot away fifty arrows; and they all stuck in the Demon's hair. The Demon snapped them all off short, and threw them down at his feet; then came up to the Bodhisatta, who drew his sword and struck the Demon, threatening him in the while. His sword — it was three-and-thirty inches long — stuck in the Demon's hair ! The Bodhisatta struck him with his spear — that stuck too ! He struck him with his club — and that stuck too !

When the Bodhisatta saw that this had stuck fast, he addressed the Demon. "You, Demon!" said he, "did you never hear of me before — the Prince of the Five Weapons ? When I came into the forest which you live in I did not trust to my bow and other weapons : This day I will pound you and grind you to powder !" Thus did he declare his resolve, and with a shout he hit at the Demon with his right hand. It stuck fast in his hair ! He hit him with his left hand — that stuck too !' With his right foot he kicked him — that stuck too; then with his left — and that stuck too ! Then he butted at him with his head, crying, "I'll pound you to powder ! " and his head stuck fast like the rest.

Thus the Bodhisatta was five times snared, caught fast in five places, hanging suspended, yet felt no fear — he was not even nervous.

Thought the Demon to himself : "Here's a lion of a man ! A noble man ! More than man is he ! Here he is, caught by a Demon like me; yet he will not fear a bit. Since I have ravaged this road, I never saw such a man. Now, why is it that he does not fear ?" He was powerless to eat the man, but asked him : "Why is it, young sir, that you are not frightened to death ?"

"Why should I fear, Demon?" replied he. "In one life a man can die but once. Besides, in my belly is a thunderbolt; if you eat me, you will never be able to digest it; this will tear your inwards into little bits, and kill you, so we shall both perish. That is why I fear nothing." (By this, the Bodhisatta meant the weapon of knowledge which he had within him.)

He had learned the only worthwhile weapon is the intelligence inside, not the weapons of the world outside. And with this weapon—his intelligence—he also knew that destroying life brings only suffering to the killer.

When he heard this reply, the Demon thought : "This young man speaks the truth. A piece of the flesh of such a lion-man as he would be too much for me to digest, if it were no bigger than a kidney-bean. I'll let him go !" So, fearing his own death, he let go the Bodhisatta, saying :

"Young sir, you are a lion of a man ! I will not eat you up. I set you free from my hands, as the moon is disgorged from the jaws of Rahu after the eclipse. Go back to the company of your friends and relations !"

And the Bodhisatta said: "Demon, I will go, as you say. You were born a Demon, cruel, blood-bibbing, devourer of the flesh and gore of others, because you did wickedly in former lives. If you still go on doing wickedly, you will go from darkness to darkness. But now that you have seen me you will find it impossible to do wickedly. Taking the life of living creatures causes birth, as an animal, in the world of *Petas* (Hungry ghosts), or, in the body of an *Asura* (Demigod), or, if one is reborn as a man, it makes his life short." **With this and the like admonitions, he told him the disadvantage of the five kinds of wickedness, and the profit of the five kinds of virtue, and frightened the Demon in various ways, discoursing to him until he subdued him, made him self-denying, and established him in the five kinds of virtue.**

Prince of FiveWeapons continued to teach the demon. Eventually, the monster agreed to follow the Five Training Steps and having carefully admonished him he made him worship the deity to whom offerings were made in that wood. In this way he transformed him from a monster into a friendly forest fairy. And when he left the forest, the prince told the local people about the change in the one-time demon. From then on they fed him regularly and lived in peace.

He then went on to Varanasi, armed with his five weapons. Afterwards he became king, and ruled righteously; and after giving alms and doing good he passed away according to his deeds.

And the Teacher, when this tale was ended, became perfectly enlightened, and repeated this verse:

One whose mind and heart from all desire is free, one who seeks for peace by living virtuously, he in due time will sever all the bonds that bind him fast to life, and cease to be.

Thus the Teacher reached the summit, through sainthood and the teaching of the law, and thereupon he declared the Four Truths. At the end of the declaring of the Truths, this Brother also attained sainthood. Then the Teacher made the connection, and gave the key to the tale, saying: "At that time Angulimala was the Demon, but the, Prince of the Five Weapons was I myself."

Insight: *Be prepared for life – don't spare yourself any pains in training and preparation. And once you have thus armed yourself – be decisive and never hesitate or give up in the face of difficulties. If you don't fear, nothing can harm you. But you have to base your fearlessness on solid training and preparedness like arming yourself with the right tools and mastering their use. This will boost your faith in yourself, which should go a long way in making yourself invincible by combating any inherent fear – this fearlessness, self-confidence and trust in your own self-worth will eventually help you in conquering all the demons in your life.*

Even if at times we feel stuck and defeated, if we are well prepared for the difficult times we will be able to say like the Bodhisatta "in my belly there is thunderbolt" by which, the story tells us, the Bodhisatta meant, "the weapon of knowledge which he had within him."

But don't depend on external weapons. The most valuable and priceless weapon you need is hidden inside uou: your own intelligence and your innate abilities; you can accomplish wonders if you cultivate them.

2nd Insight: *the highlighted passage on page 45 brings another insight : You can influence even someone as bad and mean as a demon! Never give up on anyone!! The Bodhisatta preached to the demon so much about the disadvantages of evil and advantages of virtue that he managed to bring about a change in behaviour. He discoursed " until he subdued him (the demon) and made him self-denying, and established him in the five kinds of virtue; he made him worship the deity... ... in that wood" !!! That's no mean achievement.*

6

The Great Monkey King

One day in Jetavana monastery *bhikkhus* (mendicant monks) began talking about the good that the Buddha did for his relatives. When the Buddha asked them about their subject, and they told him, he said, "*Bhikkhus*, this is not the first time the Tathagata has done good works to benefit his relatives." Then he told this story of the past.

Long, long ago, when Brahmadatta was reigning in Varanasi, the Bodhisatta was born as a monkey in the Himalayas. When he was fully grown, he was extremely strong and vigorous and became the leader of a troop of eighty thousand monkeys.

On the bank of the Ganges there was an enormous mango tree, with two massive branches so thick with leaves it looked like a mountain. Its sweet fruit was of exquisite fragrance and flavour. One branch spread over the bank of the river, but the other extended over the water. One day, while the monkey king was eating the succulent fruit, he thought, "If any of this fruit ever fell into the river, great danger could come to us." To prevent this, he ordered the monkeys to pick all the mango flowers or tiny fruit from that branch. One fruit, however, was hidden by an ant's nest and escaped the monkeys' attention. When it ripened, it fell into the river.

At that time, the King of Varanasi was bathing and amusing himself in the river. Whenever the king bathed in the river, he had nets stretched both upstream and downstream from where he was. The mango floated down the river and stuck in the net upstream from the king. That evening, as the king was leaving, the fishermen pulled in the net and found the fruit. As they had never seen a fruit like this before, they showed it to the king.

"What is this fruit?" the king asked.

"We do not know, sire," they answered.

"Who will know?"

"The foresters, sire."

The king summoned the foresters, who told him that the fruit was a mango. The king cut it with a knife and, after having the foresters eat some, tasted it himself. He also gave some of the fruit to the ministers and to his wives.

The king could not forget the magnificent flavour of the ripe mango. Obsessed with desire for the new fruit, he called the foresters again and asked where the tree stood. When he learned that it was on the bank of the river, he had many rafts joined together and sailed upstream to find it. In due course, the king and his retinue arrived at the site of the huge tree.

The king went ashore and set up a camp. After having eaten some of the delectable mangoes, he retired for the night on a bed prepared at the foot of the tree. Fires were lit and guards set on each side.

At midnight, after the men had fallen asleep and all was quiet, the monkey king came with his troop. The eighty thousand monkeys moved from branch to branch eating mangoes. The noise woke the king, who roused his archers.

"Surround those monkeys eating mangoes and shoot them," he ordered. "Tomorrow we will dine on mango fruit and monkey's flesh."

The archers readied their bows to obey the king. The monkeys saw the archers and realised that all means of escape had been cut off. Shivering in fear of death, they ran to their leader and cried, "Sire, there are men with bows all around the tree preparing to shoot us. What can we do?"

"Do not fear," he comforted them. "I will save your lives." Then he climbed onto the branch stretching over the river. Springing from the end of it, he jumped a hundred bow-lengths and landed on the opposite bank of the Ganges. Judging the distance he had jumped, he thought, "That is how far I came." Then he found a long vine and cut it, thinking, "This much will be fastened to a tree, and this much will go across the river." He secured one end of the vine to a sturdy tree and the other around his own waist. Then he again leapt across the river with the speed of a cloud blown by the wind. In his calculation, however, he had forgotten to include the length to be tied around his own waist, so he could not reach the trunk of the mango tree. He reached out and grabbed the end of a branch firmly with both hands. He signalled to the troop of monkeys and cried, "Quick! Step on my back and run along this vine to safety. Good luck to you all!"

The eighty thousand monkeys, each in turn, respectfully saluted the monkey king, asked his pardon, and escaped in this way. The last monkey in the troop, however, had long resented the leader and wished to overthrow him. When he saw the monkey king hanging there, he exulted, "This is my chance to see the last of my enemy!"

Climbing onto a high branch, he flung himself down on the monkey king's back with a dreadful blow that broke his heart. Having caused his rival excruciating pain, the wicked monkey triumphantly escaped and left the monkey king to suffer alone.

Having seen all that had happened as he lay on his bed, the king thought, "This noble monkey king, not caring for his own life, has ensured the safety of his troop. It would be wrong to destroy such an animal. I will have him brought down and taken care of." He ordered his men to lower the monkey gently down to a raft on the Ganges. After the monkey had been brought ashore and washed, the king anointed him with the purest oil. Spreading an oiled skin on his own bed and laying the monkey king on it, the king covered him with a yellow robe. After the noble animal had been given sugared water to drink, the king himself took a low seat and addressed him, "Noble monkey, you made yourself a bridge for all the other monkeys to pass over to safety. What are you to them, and what are they to you?" he asked.

The monkey explained, "Great king, I guard the herd. I am their lord and chief. When they were filled with fear of your archers, I leapt a great distance to save them. After I had tied a vine around my waist, I returned to this mango tree. My strength was almost gone, but I managed to hold the branch so that my monkeys could pass over my back and reach safety. Because I could save them, I have no fear of death. Like a righteous king, I could guarantee the happiness of those over whom I used to reign.

Sire, understand this truth! If you wish to be a righteous ruler, the happiness of your kingdom, your cities, and your people must be dear to you. It must be dearer than life itself."

After teaching the king in this way, the monkey king died. The king gave orders that the monkey king should be given a royal funeral. He ordered his wives to carry torches to the cemetery with their hair dishevelled. The ministers sent a hundred wagon loads of wood for the funeral pyre. When the regal ceremony was over, the ministers took the skull to the king. The king built a shrine at the monkey's burial place, and made offerings of incense and flowers. He had the skull inlaid with gold, raised on a spear, and carried in front of the procession returning to Varanasi. There he put it at the royal gate and paid homage to it with incense and flowers. The whole city was decorated, and the skull was honoured for seven days. For the rest of his life the king revered the skull as a relic, offering incense and garlands. Established in the wonderful teaching of the monkey king, he gave alms and performed other good deeds. He ruled his kingdom righteously and became destined for heaven.

After the lesson, the Buddha declared the Truths and said, "At that time the king was Ananda, the monkey retinue was this assembly, the wicked monkey was Devadatta, and I myself was the monkey king."

> ***Insight:*** *When you turn your life into one of service, whatever you do becomes its own reward. Even if there are some who don't appreciate your work, turn jealous and conspire against you, there will be many who will profit and benefit from your selfless acts, many of them perhaps even unknown to you because when others follow your example you become their role model.*
>
> *As the monkey king said, if you have a position with subordinates under you, their well-being is paramount to you, even "dearer than life itself," " If you are righteous." The fact that you succeed in bringing happiness to many can in turn bring happiness to you and more fulfillment than the normal remuneration earned for a job.*

7

The Strong-minded Snake

Once upon a time there was a doctor who was an expert at treating snake-bites. One day he was called for by the relatives of a man who had been bitten by a deadly poisonous snake.

The doctor told them, "There are two ways of treating this snake-bite. One is by giving medicine. The other is by capturing the snake who bit him, and forcing him to suck out his own poison." The family said, "We would like to find the snake and make him suck the poison out."

After the snake was caught, the doctor asked him, "Did you bite this man?" "Yes I did," said the snake. "Well then," said the doctor, "You must suck your own poison out of the wound." But the strong-willed snake replied, "Take back my own poison? Never! I have never done such a thing and I never will!"

Then the doctor started a wood fire and said to the snake, "If you don't suck that poison out, I'll throw you in this fire and burn you up!"

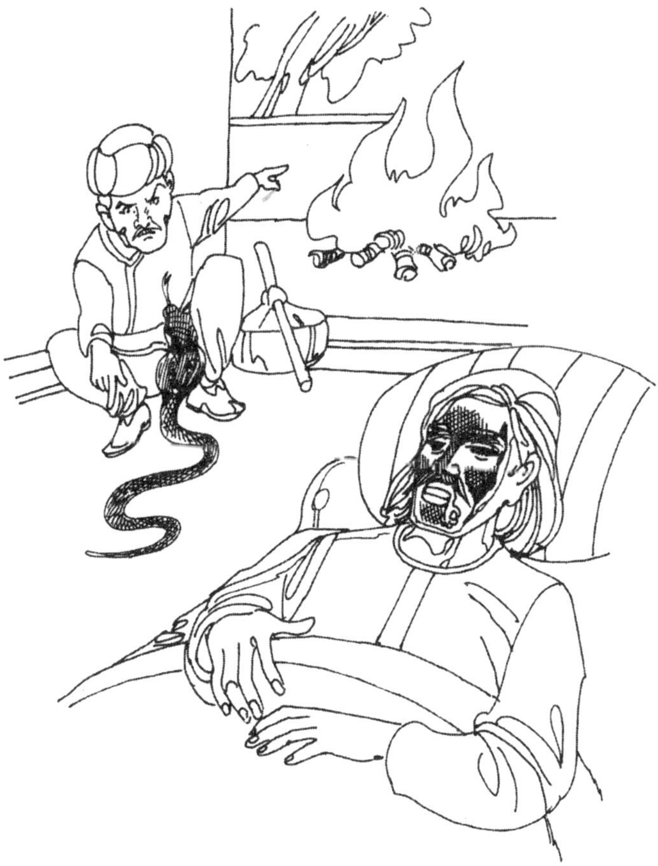

But the snake had made up his mind. He said, "I'd rather die!" And he began moving towards the fire.

In all his years, the snake-bite expert doctor had never seen anything like this! He took pity on the courageous snake, and kept him from entering the flames. He used his medicines and magic spells to remove the poison from the suffering man.

The doctor admired the snake's single-minded determination. He knew that if he used his determination in a wholesome way he could improve himself. So he taught him the Five Training Steps to avoid unwholesome actions. Then he set him free and said, "Go in peace and harm no one."

Insight: *Determination wins respect. But the key is to use it in a wholesome way.*

If your actions are not wholesome, determination can be interpreted as stubbornness and hard-headedness. So discernment is an essential ability lending value to your determination.

2nd Insight: *Always atick by your decisions and you will be appreciated for it – a wavering person does not come across as really serious and fails to impress others.*

8

A Gang of Drunkards

When Brahmadatta was king, the Enlightenment Being was born in a wealthy family. He became the richest man in Varanasi.

There also happened to be a gang of drunkards who roamed about the streets. All they ever thought about was finding ways to get alcohol, the drug they thought they couldn't live without.

One day, when they had run out of money as usual, they came up with a scheme to rob the richest man in Vanarasi. But they didn't realise that he was the reborn Bodhisatta, so he wouldn't be so easy to fool!

They decided to make a 'Mickey Finn', which is a drink of liquor with a sleeping drug secretly added to it. Their plan was to get the rich man to drink the Mickey Finn. Then when he fell asleep, they would rob all his money, jewellery, and even the rich clothes he wore. So they set up a temporary little roadside bar. They put their last remaining liquor into a bottle, and mixed in it some strong sleeping pills.

Later the rich man came by on his way to the palace. One of the alcoholics called out to him, "Honourable sir, why not start your day right—by having a drink with us? And the first one is on the house!" Then he poured a glass of the spurious liquor.

But the Enlightenment Being did not drink any form of alcohol. Nevertheless, he wondered why these drunkards were being so generous with their favourite drug. It just wasn't like them.

He realised it must be some kind of trick. So he decided to teach them a lesson. He said, "It would be an insult to appear before the king in a drunken state, or with even the slightest smell of liquor on my breath. But please be so kind as to wait for me here. I'll see you again when I return from the palace."

The drunkards were disappointed. They would not be able to drink again as soon as they wanted. But they decided to be patient and wait.

Later that day the rich man came back to the little roadside bar. The alcoholics were getting desperate for a drink. They called him over and said, "Honourable sir, why not celebrate your visit to the king? Have a drink of this fine liquor. Remember, the first one is free!"

But the rich man just kept looking at the liquor bottle and glass. He said, "I don't trust you. That bottle and glass of liquor are exactly as they were this morning. If it were as good as you say it is, you would have tasted some yourselves by now. In fact, you couldn't help but drink it all! I'm no fool. You must have added another drug to the alcohol."

The richest man in Varanasi went on his way, and the gang of drunkards went back to their plotting and scheming.

Insight: *Stay sober and use your common sense at all times. These two things can mean the difference between life and death.*

Deceit and cunning will not catch by surprise those who stay on guard and attentive to detail. There are enough crooks and confidence tricksters around to permit and tempt you to lower your guard and fall prey to their wiles.

Those who allow themselves to get under the influence of any substances is handing over control of their life, (even if for a short period of time) to another and the enemy can take advantage of this situation. If one is a habitual offender the risks are even higher because whoever wants to take advantage of such a person, can watch and observe the details of where and when one indulges in consuming such substances and then plot and plan the hour of strike !!

9

A Huge Lump of Gold

Once there was a rich village. Some wealthy villager decided to hide a huge lump of gold to protect it from bandits and robbers. So he buried it in a nearby rice field.

Many years later, the village was no longer rich, and the rice field was abandoned and unused. A poor farmer decided to plow the field. After ploughing it for sometime, it so happened that his left leg struck the long forgotten buried treasure.

At first he thought it must be a very hard tree root. But when he uncovered it, he saw that it was beautiful shining gold. Since it was daytime he was afraid to try and take it with him. So he covered it up again and waited for nightfall.

The poor farmer returned in the middle of the night. Again he uncovered the golden treasure. He tried to lift it, but it was too heavy. He tied ropes around it and tried to drag it. But it was so huge he couldn't budge it an inch. He became frustrated, thinking he was lucky to find a treasure, and unlucky not to be able to take it with him.

He even tried kicking the huge lump of gold. But again it wouldn't budge an inch!

Then he sat down and began to consider the situation. He decided the only thing to do was to break the lump of gold into four smaller lumps. Then he could carry home one piece at a time.

He thought, "One lump I will use for ordinary day-to-day living. The second lump I will save for a rainy day. The third lump I will invest in my farming business. And I will gain merit with the fourth lump by giving it to the poor and needy and for other good works."

With a calm mind he divided the huge lump of gold into these four smaller lumps. Then it was easy to carry them home on four separate trips.

Afterwards he lived happily.

Insight: *"Don't bite off more than you can chew." No task is too large if you divide your work into sufficiently small chunks that you can handle easily. One at a time. Before you know it, the task will be accomplished. There is a popular riddle in management circles which illustrates this truth: How do you eat an elephant? Answer: Slice by slice. So also can any difficult target be reached: by sub-dividing or cutting down a gigantic plan into manageable-sized blocks.*

2nd Insight: *Plan your finances and wealth if you want to live happily. And that involves a lot of right decisions. Where do you store your lump of gold ? Do you sell a part of it or do you wait for a better price? Am I knowledgeable enough to take all these decisions or do I need some expert help? How to find the right expert who is really knowledgeable? – Decisions ... Decisions*

10

A Prince of Monkeys

A cruel monkey king ruled in the Himalayas. All the monkeys in his band were his own wives and children. He was afraid that one of his sons might grow up and take over as king. So it was his policy to bite each son just after he was born. This altered him so he would be too weak to ever challenge his father.

A wife of the monkey king was pregnant. Just in case the unborn one was a son, she wanted to protect him from the cruel policy of her husband. So she ran away into a forest at the foot of a distant mountain. There she soon gave birth to a bright little baby boy monkey.

Before long this baby grew up to be big and strong. One day he asked his mother, "Where is my father?" She told him, "He is king of a band of monkeys living at the foot of a far-off mountain. That makes you a prince!"

The Prince of monkeys said, "Kindly take me to my father." His mother said, "No my son, I am afraid to do so. Your father bites all his sons in order to weaken them for life. He is afraid that one of his sons will replace him as king." The Prince said, "Don't be afraid for me, mother. I can take care of myself." This gave her confidence, so she agreed and took him to his father.

When the cruel old king saw his strong young son, he thought. "I have no doubt that when this my son grows stronger, he will take away my kingdom from me. Therefore, I must kill him while I still can! I will hug him, pretending it is out of love for him. But really I will squeeze him to death!"

The king welcomed his son, saying, "Ah, my long lost son! Where have you been all this time? I have missed you dearly." Then he took him in his arms and hugged him. He kept squeezing harder and harder, trying to squeeze the life out of him! But the Prince of monkeys was as strong as an elephant. He hugged his father right back. He squeezed him tighter and tighter, until he could feel the old king's rib bones starting to crack!

After this terrible greeting, the monkey king got even more terrified that one day his son would kill him. He thought, "Nearby there is a pond possessed by a water demon. It would be easy to get him to eat my son. Then my problems would be over!"

The monkey king said, "Oh my dear son, now is the perfect time for you to come home. For I am old and I would like to hand over my band of monkeys to you. But I need flowers for the coronation ceremony. Go to the nearby pond and bring back two kinds of white water lilies, three kinds of blue water lilies and five types of lotuses."

The Prince of monkeys said, "Yes my father, I will go and get them."

When he arrived at the pond, he saw that there were many kinds of water lilies and lotuses growing all over it. But instead of jumping right in and picking them, he investigated carefully. He walked slowly along the bank. He noticed there were footprints going into the pond, but none coming out! After considering, he realised this was a sure sign that the pond was possessed by a water demon. He also realised his father must have sent him there to be killed.

He investigated further, until he found a narrow part of the pond. There, with great effort, he was able to jump from one side clear across to the other. In the midst of his leap he reached down and picked flowers, without actually getting into the water. Then he jumped back again, picking more flowers. He continued jumping back and forth, collecting lots of flowers.

Suddenly, the water demon stuck his head up above the water. He exclaimed, "In all the time I've lived here I have never seen anyone, man or beast, as wise as this monkey! He has picked all the flowers he wanted, without ever coming within the grasp of my power, here in my kingdom of water."

Then the ferocious demon made a path for himself through the water and came up onto the bank. He said, "My lord, king of monkeys, there are three qualities that make a person unbeatable by his enemies. It appears that you have all three—skill, courage and wisdom. You must be truly invincible! Tell me, mighty one, why have you collected all those flowers?"

The Prince of monkeys replied, "My father wants to make me king in his place. He sent me to gather these flowers for the coronation ceremony."

The water demon said, "You are too noble to be burdened by carrying these flowers. Let me carry them for you." He picked up all the flowers and followed him.

From a distance, the monkey king saw the water demon carrying the flowers and following the prince. He thought, "I sent him to get flowers, thinking he would be eaten by the demon. But instead he has made the water demon his servant. I am lost!"

The monkey king was afraid all his unwholesome deeds had caught up with him. He went into a sudden panic, which caused his heart to break into seven pieces. Of course, this killed him on the spot!

The monkey band voted to make the strong young prince the new king.

***Insight:** It pays to be careful in all circumstances. You never know in today's competitive world who is against you and determined to undermine your interests. In such circumstances you need all the skills, courage and wisdom that you can get. In order to come out a winner the young monkey had to prove both his physical strength as well as his ingenuity .*

***2nd insight :** Our deeds form our karma and seal our kismet (luck). So make righteousness and wholesomeness the key principles in your daily life. With every step and move we weave the cloak of our destiny.*

11

The Green Wood Gatherer

Once there was a world-famous teacher and holy man in the city of Takxasila. He had 500 students training under him.

One day these 500 young men went into the forest to gather firewood. One of them came upon a tree with no leaves. He thought, "How lucky I am! This tree must be dead and dry, perfect for firewood. I'll take a nap while the others are busy searching in the woods. When it's time to return, it will be easy to climb this tree and break off branches for firewood. So what's the hurry?" He spread his jacket on the ground, lay down on it, and fell fast asleep - snoring loudly.

After a while all the other students began carrying their bundles of firewood back to Takxasila. On their way they passed the snoring sleeper. They kicked him to wake him up and said, "Wake up! Wake up! It's time to return to our teacher."

The lazy student woke up suddenly and rubbed his eyes. Still not fully awake, he climbed up the tree. He began breaking off branches and discovered that they were actually still green, not dry at all.

While he was breaking one of them, it snapped back and poked him in the eye. From then on he had to hold his eye with one hand while he finished gathering his bundle of green wood. Then he carried it back to Takxasila, running to catch up. He was the last one back, and threw his bundle on top of the rest.

Meanwhile, an invitation arrived to a religious ceremony. It was to be held the next day at a remote village. The holy man told his 500 pupils, "This will be good training for you. You will have to eat an early breakfast tomorrow morning. Then go to the village for the religious service. When you return, bring back my share of the offerings as well as your own."

The students awoke early the next morning. They awakened the school cook and asked her to prepare porridge for their breakfast. She went out in the dark to the woodpile. She picked up the top bundle of the lazy man's green wood. She brought it inside and tried to start her cooking fire. But even though she blew and blew on it, she couldn't get the fire going. The wood was too green and damp.

When the sun came up there was still no fire for cooking breakfast. The students said, "It's getting to be too late to go to the village." So off they went to their teacher.

The teacher asked them, "Why are you still here? Why haven't you left yet?" They told him, "A lazy good-for-nothing slept while we all worked. He climbed a tree and poked himself in the eye. He gathered only green wood and threw it on top of the woodpile. This was picked up by the school cook. Because it was green and damp, she couldn't get the breakfast fire started. And now it's too late to go to the village."

The world-famous teacher said, "A fool who is lazy causes trouble for everyone. When what should be done early is put off until later, it is soon regretted."

Insight: *Don't delay what you have to do for another day or even for another hour. If you indulge in laziness and procrastination, the work tends to mount and you are unable to cope with it, often resulting in a hurried, last minute and badly done job. The consequences of such a situation overwhelm you and others around you.*

In order to avoid putting ourselves into such a situation and victimising those around us(colleagues, friends and family members) who are affected by our actions, it is necessary to take a decision right at the outset. When we undertake a job or accept any responsibilities, we would be keeping up our will to do our duties as they arise –this would leave us the time to accomplish the seemingly impossible, and do a well done job for that.

12

Two Mothers

Once upon a time there was a very well-known teacher in the city of Takxasila, in northern India. He taught religion, as well as all other subjects. His knowledge was enormous and his teaching ability made him world famous.

At that time a son was born to a rich family in Varanasi. The family kept a holy fire burning constantly from that day on. When the son turned 16, they gave him a choice. They said, "This holy fire has been burning since your birth. If you wish to be reborn in a high heaven world, take it into the forest and worship the fire god."

"However, if you wish to live the home life of a family man, you must learn how to manage the wealth of our family in the affairs of the world. If that is the life you choose, go and study under the world famous teacher of Takxasila."

The young man said, "I don't want to be a holy man. I would much rather be a family man. Then I will be happy for the rest of my life." So his parents sent him to the world famous teacher. They gave him a thousand gold coins to pay for his lessons.

After several years the man graduated with honours and returned home to Varanasi.

Meanwhile, his parents had come to wish more and more that he would become a holy man in the forest. This was just as they had wished on the day he was born. His mother wanted the best life possible for her son. She thought, "My son wants to marry and raise a family. He does not realise how dangerous a wicked woman can be to a man. I must find a way to get his teacher to teach him this."

So the wise woman asked her son, "Did you earn only the Ordinary Degree without also obtaining the higher Unhappiness Degree?" Her son replied, "I have earned only the Ordinary Degree."

His mother said, "How can you be called educated in the ways of the world if you have learned nothing about unhappiness? Return to the great teacher and ask for the Unhappiness Degree." The son dutifully followed his good mother's advice and returned to Takxasila.

It just so happened that the world famous teacher had a mother who was 120 years old. She was blind and very weak. The teacher bathed and fed and cared for her with his own hands. Since it took more and more of his time, he was forced to give up teaching. He and his mother moved into a forest hut where he looked after her, night and day.

When the young student arrived from Varanasi he found that his old teacher was no longer at the college. Hearing that he had retired to the forest, he went and found him there.

After greeting each other, the teacher asked him, "Why have you come back so soon?" He replied, "Honourable professor, you did not give me the Unhappiness Degree." "Who told you about that degree?" asked the teacher. "My mother, sir," he said.

The teacher thought, "I've never heard of such a degree! No doubt his wise mother wanted me to teach him how wicked some women can be. For they bring great unhappiness to men."

He said, "All right, I will teach you so you can earn this high degree. The course is a work-study programme. Your lessons will consist of taking care of my old mother for me. You will bathe, feed and care for her tenderly with your own hands."

"While you are washing and massaging her body, you must say, 'Dear lady, even in your old age your skin remains fair and beautiful.' You must constantly exaggerate her beauty in this way, saying, 'When you were young, you must have been even more beautiful!' And if she says anything to you, you must tell me without shame, whatever it is, hiding nothing."

"If you do these things correctly, you will earn the Unhappiness Degree. Then your mother will be proud of you."

The student agreed and began tending to the 120-year-old lady. He bathed and fed her with his own hands. He massaged her arms, legs, back and head. While doing this he said, "Madam, it is marvellous indeed! Even in such great old age, your arms and legs are so very beautiful! I can guess how beautiful you were in your youth!" In this way he exaggerated her beauty again and again, for many days.

Gradually, desire began to arise in the old lady's mind. Even though she knew she was blind and her body was rotten from old age, she thought, "No doubt this young man would like to live with me like a husband." So she asked him, "Do you want to be with me, just like a husband and wife?"

The man replied, "Oh yes, of course, madam. I want to very much. But how can I? Your son is my teacher and he is very respectable. It would cause such a scandal! I will not dishonour my teacher."

Then the teacher's mother said, "Well in that case, if you really want to be with me, then kill my son!"

The student said, "How can I kill him when I have been studying with him for so long? How can I kill him just because of this desire for you?" Then she said, "If you will stay with me and not desert me, I will kill him myself!"

As he had agreed, the student went to the world famous teacher and told him all that had taken place. Amazingly, the teacher did not seem surprised. He said, "You have done well to tell me this, my pupil. I appreciate your good work."

Then he examined his mother's horoscope and discovered that this was to be the day of her death. He said, "I will arrange a test for her."

The teacher carved a statue from the softwood of a tree limb. He made it look exactly like himself, life-size. He laid it in his own bed and pulled the sheet up over it. He attached a long string to it and gave it to his pupil. He told him, "Now take this string and axe to my mother. Tell her it is time to do the killing."

Obediently the student returned to the blind old lady. He said, "Madam, my master is sleeping in his bed. If you follow this string it will lead you to him. Then kill him with this axe, if you really can do such a thing!"

She replied, "If you do not abandon me, I will do it." He said, "Why should I abandon you?"

Then she took the axe in her hands. She trembled as she stood up. Slowly she followed the string to her son's bed. She felt the statue and thought she recognised her son. She pulled down the sheet from the head and raised the axe. Thinking to kill him with one blow she struck the neck as hard as she could with the axe. But it made a thumping sound, so she knew it had struck wood.

The teacher asked, "What are you doing, my mother?" Suddenly she realised she had been deceived and discovered. The shock was so overwhelming that she dropped dead on the spot! This time the horoscope had been correct.

The world famous teacher respectfully burned his mother's body and offered flowers on her ashes.

Then he said to his pupil, "My son, there really is no such thing as the 'Unhappiness Degree'. Wicked women cause unhappiness. You are fortunate to have such a good and wise mother. By sending you here to earn the Unhappiness Degree, she wanted you to learn how evil some women can be.

"You have seen with your own eyes how my mother was filled with craving and vanity. She has taught you this lesson. Now return to your wise mother, who cares so much for your well-being."

When he arrived home his mother asked, "My dear son, have you finally earned the high degree in the subject of Unhappiness?" He replied, "Yes mother."

Then she said, "I ask you again, my son, do you wish to leave the worldly life and go into the forest to worship the fire god? Or do you wish to marry and lead the family life?"

Her son replied, "I do not wish to lead the family life. I have seen with my own eyes how evil some women can be. There is no limit to their craving and vanity. Therefore I want nothing to do with family life. I will seek peace as a forest monk."

He respectfully took leave of his parents. After many years of peaceful meditation in the forest, he eventually died and was reborn in a high heaven world.

Insight1: *The choice between a family life and a religious life is an important one and the decision can be taken only after exposure to the world and full knowledge of the risks involved in undertaking an intimate relationship. The moment one graduates may not be the right time to take such an important decision.*

It takes time to become knowledgeable in the ways of the world and to learn to accept some hard facts like the one brought out by the story: that lust and craving can interfere with the reasoning abilities of even an intelligent person and blind him/her to the most cherished values, totally destroying the life of a family. It's a tough decision – an ideal family life holds naturally a strong attraction to most people BUT do we have the strength to tide over the storms and stresses which invariable attack the life of any family or would we rather renounce family life for a different one?

Insight 2: *Educational degrees are no substitute for experience of the world. You need both to make the right choices and decisions, and to succeed in the world and be happy.*

13

The Wicked Lady and the Buttermilk Wise Man

Once a very rich man was living in Varanasi. He had a daughter who was one of the most beautiful women in the city. Her skin was as soft as rose petals, her complexion was like lotus blossoms, and her hair was as black as midnight. But unfortunately her beauty was only skin deep. For, on the inside, she was very cruel. She insulted her servants and even enjoyed beating them. She became known as the 'Wicked Lady'.

One day she went down to the river for her bath. While she bathed, her servant girls played and splashed in the water. Suddenly, it became dark and a heavy rainstorm came upon them. Most of the attendants and guards ran away. The servant girls said to each other, "This would be a perfect time to get rid of the Wicked Lady once and for all!" So they deserted her there, still bathing in midstream. The storm became more and more terrible as the sun set.

When the servant girls arrived home without the Wicked Lady, the rich man asked them, "Where is my precious daughter?" They replied, "We saw her coming out of the river, but since then we haven't seen her. We don't know where she went." The rich man sent out relatives to search for her, but she was nowhere to be found. Meanwhile, the Wicked Lady had been swept downstream by the ferocious flooded river.

A holy man was living in the forest next to the river. In this peaceful area he had been meditating for a long time, until he had come to enjoy the inner happiness of a high mental state. Because of this happiness, he was quite sure he had left the ordinary desires of the world behind.

At about midnight the Wicked Lady was carried past the holy man's hut by the raging river. She was crying out and screaming for help. When he heard her, the holy man realised a woman was in danger. So he took a torch down to the river and saw her being swept along. He dived in and saved her. He comforted her, saying, "Don't worry, I'll look after you."

He carried her into his hut and made a fire to dry her off and warm her up. He gave her fruits to eat. When she had eaten her fill, he asked, "Where do you live? How did you fall in the river?" She told him about the storm and how her servants deserted her. He took pity on her and let her sleep in his hut for the next couple of nights. He himself slept under the stars.

When she had recovered her strength, he told her it was time to return home. But she knew that he was the type of holy man who promised never to live with a woman, as husband and wife. That was why he had slept outside while she slept in the hut.

Just to prove her own power and superiority over him, she decided to seduce him into breaking his religious promise. She refused to leave until she had tricked him into falling in love with her.

The Wicked Lady used the poses and tricks and flatteries that women learn. The holy man was not yet strong enough to resist her tempting ways. After a few days she succeeded in seducing him into breaking his promise. They began living together in the quiet forest as if they were husband and wife. He lost the inner happiness he had gained by years of meditating.

But soon the Wicked Lady grew bored with forest life. She missed the noise and excitement of a crowded city life. So she cooed and coaxed until she got her way, and they moved to a nearby village.

In the beginning, the holy man supported her by selling buttermilk. Later on, the villagers came and asked him for advice. They soon realised that listening to him brought good fortune. So they started calling him 'the Buttermilk Wise Man', and gave him a hut to live in.

Then one day a gang of bandits attacked the village. They robbed all the valuables and kidnapped some of the villagers, including the Wicked Lady. When they got to their forest hide-out they divided up the loot. When they began dividing up the prisoners, the bandit chief was attracted by the Wicked Lady's great beauty. So he took her for himself as a wife.

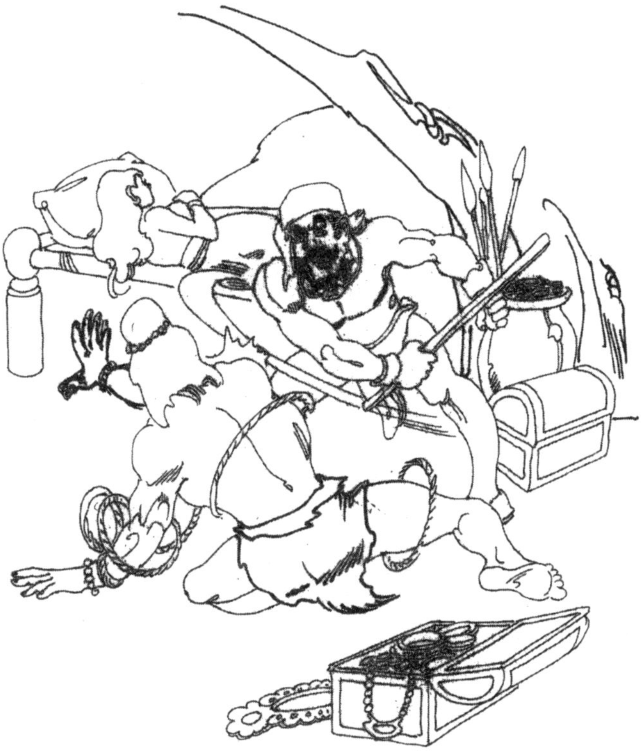

All the other prisoners were soon released. When they returned to the village, the Buttermilk Wise Man asked what happened to his wife. They told him she had been kept as wife by the bandit chief. He thought, “She will never be able to live without me. She will find a way to escape and come back to me.” Deciding the village was now unlucky, all the others left it. But the Buttermilk Wise Man remained in his hut, convinced that his wife would return.

Lo and behold, the Wicked Lady enjoyed the exciting life of bandits. But she worried that her husband would come and take her back. She thought, “Then I would lose all my newfound luxuries. I would be safer if I got rid of him. Therefore, I will send him a letter, pretending to be deeply in love with him. Just as before I will use my power of seduction to cause his downfall. But this time he will meet his death, and I will remain the bandit queen!"

When the Buttermilk Wise Man received the letter he believed every word. He rushed into the forest and ran to the gang's hideout. When he called out to her, the Wicked Lady came out and said, "Oh my lord and master, I'm so happy to see you. I can hardly wait to escape with you. But now is not a good time. The bandit chief could easily follow us and kill us both. So let us wait until nightfall." She took him inside, fed him, and hid him in a closet.

When the chief returned in the evening he was drunk. The Wicked Lady asked him, "My lord and chief, if you saw my former husband now, what would you do?" "I would beat him up and kick him from one side of the room to the other!" he bragged, "Where is he now?" "He is much closer than you think," she said, "In fact, he is right here in this closet!"

He opened the door and dragged out the Buttermilk Wise Man. He proceeded to beat him up and kick him around the room, just as he had boasted. His poor victim did not cry out. He only muttered –

"Ungrateful hater, Lying traitor."

That was all he said. It seemed he was finally learning a lesson—but so painfully!

Eventually the drunken bandit got tired of beating him. He tied him up, ate dinner, and passed out into drunken sleep.

The next morning, after sleeping off his drunkenness, the bandit chief woke up sober. He began beating and kicking his tied up victim again. Still the Buttermilk Wise Man did not cry out, but kept on muttering - "Ungrateful hater, Lying traitor."

The bandit thought, "While I keep punishing this man, why does he keep saying the same thing over and over?" Seeing that his wife was still fast asleep, he asked him what he meant.

The Buttermilk Wise Man replied, "Listen and I will tell. I was a forest holy man, peacefully enjoying a high state of mind. One night I heard this woman crying out as she was being swept down a river in a storm. I saved her life and brought her back to health. Meanwhile, she seduced me and I lost all my inner calm and happiness. We went to live in a village and I led a very ordinary life. Then you kidnapped her. She sent me a letter saying she suffered living with you, and begged me to rescue her. So you see—she enticed me into this disaster. She put me at your mercy. That is why I say—"Ungrateful hater, Lying traitor.'"

The bandit chief was not stupid. He thought, "This man was such a good provider, and yet she has put him in this plight. What would she be capable of doing to me? It would be better to finish her off!"

He untied the Buttermilk Wise Man and comforted him, saying, "Don't worry, I'll look after you." He awakened the Wicked Lady and said, "My darling, let us kill this man right next to his own village." He took them to the boundary of the deserted village. He told her to hold her former husband. Then he raised his mighty sword and came down with it. But at the last instant he sliced the Wicked Lady in half!

Even someone as wicked as this murderous bandit can change his ways. He began by nursing his former rival back to health. After a few days of rest he asked, "What are you going to do now?"

The wise man replied, "I don't want to live as a householder anymore. I want to return to my old forest and meditate."

The bandit said, "I too would like to be ordained and learn to meditate in the forest." After giving up all his stolen goods, he went and lived in the forest with the Buttermilk Wise Man as his teacher. After much effort, they both attained a high state of inner happiness.

Insight: *Heartless greed is dangerous. Ambition is good as long as we don't victimise anyone to satiate our greed. Insatiable greed can make one behave in wicked ways and lead one to troubled days by inviting enmity and hatred into our lives. So it is advisable to rid oneself of any such traits by keeping ones wants reasonable and under control.*

If we don't nip the vice in the bud we may have to learn it the hard way—the consequences of giving in selfishly to greed, without concern for others, will eventually catch up with us. Our viciousness towards others can turn its face on us....

So if we want to keep moving upwards, without a sharp fall, we had better make sure we don't take recourse to trampling over anyone in order to grab new positions whether professionally or socially.

14

Country Man and City Wife

There was a well-known teacher who taught in and around Varanasi. He had over 500 students. One of these was from the distant countryside. Knowing little about the ways of city folks, he fell in love with a Varanasi girl and married her. After the marriage he resumed his studies with the famous teacher. But he started missing classes, sometimes staying away for two or three days at a time.

His wife was used to doing whatever she wanted. Even though she was married to the student, she was not loyal and faithful. She still had secret boy friends.

It just so happened that after she had been with a boy friend, she acted very humble with her husband. She spoke softly and tried very hard to please him. But on other days, when she had done nothing wrong, she was rude and domineering. She yelled at her husband and nagged him. This drove the man crazy. He was completely confused by how differently she acted from one day to the next.

The countryman was so disturbed that he stayed away from classes. And while he remained home he discovered that his city wife was unfaithful. He was so upset that he missed school for seven or eight days.

When he finally showed up, the famous teacher asked, "Young man, you have been away so long. What was the matter?" He replied, "Sir, my wife is cheating on me very much, and acts as humble as a servant. But on other days she is arrogant and domineering, rough and rude. I can't figure her out. I don't know what to do or where to go for help. That's why I couldn't attend your classes."

The teacher said, “Young man, don’t worry. Rivers can be bathed in by anyone, rich or poor. Highways too are open to all. Generous people build roadside rest houses to gain merit, and anyone can sleep there. Likewise, all are welcome to take water from the village well.”

“So too, there are some women who won’t be faithful to one man. They love to keep their secret boy friends. That’s just the way some people are. It’s hard to understand why they act the way they do. But why get angry about what you cannot change?”

“On the days when your wife has been with a boy friend, those are the days she acts meek and mild. But on the days when she has done nothing wrong, those are the days she acts rough and rude. That’s just the way some people are. So why get angry about what you cannot change?”

“**Accept her the way she is. Treat her in the same understanding way, whether she is kind or mean to you.** Why get angry about what you cannot change?”

“The student from the countryside followed the famous teacher’s advice. His city wife’s behaviour no longer upset him. And when she realised that her actions were no longer secret, she gave up her boyfriends and changed her ways.

***Insight:** Understanding and loving ways relieve anger. Add acceptance to it and you'll manage to bring about reform in those who proved to be incorrigible by using anger and scolding.*

The teacher was indeed wise: he convinced the husband to stop getting angry as one cannot change other people and instead he advised the husband to treat the wife well, always. Only when the husband followed the wise advice of his teacher and stopped getting angry and tried to change the wife, did she in fact change. So, because of the wisdom of the teacher the man discovered a very important truth about life: Only total acceptance of the people around us can change them and bring out the best in them. It may require a difficult decision and commitment from our part to be able to bestow on our dear ones "unconditional love and total acceptance" without admonishing them to behave in a particular way or perform well in their respective roles. But these two unconditional love and total acceptance, are extremely difficult as they, are almost unfailingly, powerful agents of transformation.

15

The Fish Who Worked A Miracle

Once the Enlightenment Being was born as a fish in a pond in northern India. There were many kinds of fish, big and small, living in the pond with the Bodhisatta.

There was a severe drought. The rainy season did not come as usual. The crops died, and many ponds, lakes and rivers dried up.

The fish and turtles dug down and buried themselves in the mud, frantically trying to keep wet and save themselves. The crows were pleased by all this. They stuck their beaks down into the mud, pulled up the frightened little fish, and feasted on them.

Thc of pain and death of other fish touched the Enlightenment Being with sadness, and filled him with pity and compassion. He realised that he was the only one who could save them. But it would take a miracle.

The truth was that he had remained innocent by never taking the life of anyone. He was determined to use the power of this wholesome truth to make rain fall from the sky, and release his relatives from their misery and death.

He pulled himself up from under the black mud. He was a big fish, and as black from the mud as polished ebony. He opened his eyes, which sparkled like rubies, looked up to the sky, and called on the rain god Pajjunna. He exclaimed, "Oh my friend Pajjunna, God of Rain, I am suffering for the sake of my relatives. Why do you withhold rain from me, who am perfectly wholesome, and make me suffer in sympathy with all these fish?"

"I was born among fish, for whom it is customary to eat other fish - even our own kind, like cannibals! But since I was born, I myself have never eaten any fish, even one as tiny as a rice grain. In fact, I have never taken life from anyone. The truthfulness of my innocence gives me the right to say to you: Make the rains fall! Relieve the suffering of my relatives!"

He said this the way one gives orders to a servant.

And he continued, commanding the mighty rain god Pajjunna: "Make rain fall from the thunderclouds! Do not allow the crows their hidden treasures! Let the crows feel the sorrow of their unwholesome actions. At the same time release me from my sorrow, who have lived in perfect wholesomeness."

After only a short pause, the sky opened up with a heavy downpour of rain, relieving many from the fear of death - fish, turtles and even humans. And when the great fish who had worked this miracle eventually died, he was reborn as he deserved.

Insight: *True innocence embodies an immense compassion for the suffering of others and a high degree of empathy bringing about a pressing need to do everything in your power to soothe such suffering.*

Remaining true to one's honourable principles of absolute non-violence can turn one into an epitome of truth and innocence and help one keep one's relationship with the Divine Being at an optimum level which, in turn, can empower one to ask for God's graces and blessings in our day-to-day needs and whenever more pressing needs arise.

2nd Insight : *One wholesome person can save hundreds who even do not have the same merit in the eyes of God.*

16

The Shovel Wise Man

Once the Enlightened Being was born into a family of vegetable gardeners. After he grew up, he cleared a patch of land with his shovel. He grew herbs, pumpkins, melons, cucumbers and other vegetables. These he sold to earn a humble living.

The shovel was his one and only possession in the whole world. He carried it in the same way a forest monk carries his walking staff. So he became known as the 'Shovel Wise Man'.

One day he thought, "What good does it do me to live the ordinary everyday life of a gardener? I will give up this life and go to meditate in the forest. Then I will be peaceful and happy." So the Shovel Wise Man hid his one possession, his shovel, and became a forest meditator.

Before too long, he started thinking about his only possession, his shovel. He was so attached to this shovel that he couldn't get it out of his mind, no matter how hard he tried! Trying to meditate seemed useless, so he gave it up. He returned to his shovel and his ordinary life as a vegetable gardener.

Lo and behold, in a little while the Shovel Wise Man again gave up the everyday life, hid his shovel and became a forest meditator.

Again he could not get his shovel out of his mind, and returned to being a gardener. All in all, this happened six times!

The next time the Shovel Wise Man gave up his forest meditation. He finally realised it was because of his old worn out shovel that he had gone back and forth seven times! So he decided to throw it away, once and for all, in a deep river. Then he would return to the forest for good.

He took his shovel down to the riverbank. He thought, "Let me not see where this shovel enters the water. Otherwise it may tempt me again to give up my quest." So he closed his eyes, swung the shovel in a circle over his head three times, and let it fly into the midst of the river. Realising that he would never be able to find the shovel again, he shouted, just like a lion roars, "I have conquered! I have conquered! I have conquered!"

It so happened that the King of Varanasi was riding by at that very moment. He was returning from putting down a revolt in a border village. He had bathed in the river, and had just seated himself on his magnificent royal elephant. He was riding back to Varanasi in a victory procession.

When he heard the triumphant shouts of the Enlightened Being, he said to his ministers, "Listen. Who is shouting and roaring, just like a lion, 'I have conquered'? Whom has he conquered? Bring that man to me!"

When they brought the Shovel Wise Man to him, the king said, "I am a conqueror because I have won a battle. You say that you have conquered. Whom did you conquer?"

The Enlightened Being replied, "Your lordship, even if you conquer a hundred thousand armies, they are meaningless victories if you still have unwholesome thoughts and desires in your own mind! By conquering the craving in my mind, I know I have won the battle against unwholesome thoughts."

As he spoke he concentrated his mind on the water in the river, then on the idea of water itself, and reached a high mental state. In a sitting position he rose into the air. He preached these words of Truth to the king: "Defeating an enemy who returns to fight you again and again is no real victory. But if you defeat the unwholesomeness in your own mind, no one can take that true victory from you!"

While the king was listening to these words, all unwholesome thoughts left his mind. It occurred to him to give up the ordinary world and seek real peace and happiness. He asked, "Where are you going now, wise one?" He answered, "I am going to the Himalayas, oh king, to practise meditation." The king said, "Please take me with you. I too wish to give up the common worldly life." Lo and behold, as the king turned northward with the Shovel Wise Man, so did the entire army and all the royal ministers and attendants.

Soon the news reached the people of Varanasi that the king and all those with him were leaving the ordinary world and following the Shovel Wise Man to the Himalayas. Then all the people in the entire city of Varanasi followed them towards the northern mountains. Varanasi was empty!

This great migration of people came to the attention of the god Sakka, King of the Heaven of 33. Never had he seen so many giving up worldly power. He ordered the architect of the gods to build a dwelling place in the Himalayan forests for all these people.

When they arrived in the Himalayas, the Shovel Wise Man was the first to announce that he had given up the ordinary world for good. Then all those with him did the same. Never was so much worldly power given up, or renounced, at the same time.

The Shovel Wise Man developed what holy men call the 'Four Heavenly States of Mind'. First is loving-kindness, tender affection for all. Second is feeling sympathy and pity for all those who suffer. Third is feeling happiness for all those who are joyful. And the fourth state is balance and calm, even in the face of difficulties or troubles.

He taught the others advanced meditation. With great effort they all gained high mental states, leading to rebirth in heavenly worlds.

Insight: *The ultimate conquest is that of your own mind – it is ultimate because it is the most difficult to achieve- freedom from unwholesome thoughts. If you can't drop your attachment to your possessions your mind is a slave to them. Even a single possession is enough to keep the mind from finding freedom, if you are attached to it. The key to mental and emotional freedom is to keep yourself detached from your possessions but if you cannot manage to do so, then only the extreme step which is getting rid of them all, can help you free your mind.*

In pursuit of such a lofty ideal it is not worth allowing any stumbling block thwart your path even if it is your last possession.

It is a difficult decision which you either take or remain forever a slave to your attachments.

17

A Motherless Son

When King Brahmadatta was ruling in Varanasi in northern India, he had a clever minister who pleased him very much. To show his appreciation he appointed him headman of a remote border village. His duty was to represent the king and collect the king's taxes from the villagers.

Before long the headman was completely accepted by the villagers. Since he had been sent by the just King Brahmadatta, they respected him highly. They came to trust him as much as if he had been born among them.

In addition to being clever, the headman was also very greedy. Collecting the king's taxes was not enough reward for him. After becoming friendly with a gang of bandits, he thought up a plan to make himself rich.

The headman said to his friends, the robbers, "I will find excuses and reasons to lead all the villagers into the jungle. This will be easy for me, since they trust me as one of their own. I will keep them busy in the jungle, while you invade the village and rob everything of value. Carry everything away before I bring the people home. In return for my help, you must give me half of all the loot!" The bandits agreed, and a date was set.

When the day arrived, the headman assembled all the villagers and led them into the jungle. According to the plan, the bandits entered the unprotected village. They stole everything of value they could find. They also killed all the defenseless village cows, and cooked and ate the meat. At the end of the day the gang collected all their stolen goods and escaped.

It just so happened that on that very same day a travelling merchant came to the village to trade his goods. When he saw the bandits he stayed out of sight.

The headman brought all the villagers home in the evening. He ordered them to make a lot of noise by beating drums as they marched towards the village. If the bandits had still been there, they would have heard the villagers coming for sure.

The village people saw that they had been robbed and all their cows were dead and partly eaten. This made them very sad. The travelling merchant appeared and said to them, 'This treacherous village headman has betrayed that trust you reposed in him. He must be a partner of the gang of bandits. Only after they left with all your valuables did he lead you home, beating drums as loudly as possible!

'This man pretends to know nothing about what has happened - as innocent as a newborn lamb! In truth, it's as if a son did something so shameful that his mother would say -'I am not his mother. He is not my son. My son is dead!"'

Before long, news of the crime reached the king. He recalled the treacherous headman and punished him according to the law.

Insight 1: *No one defends a betrayer of trust.*

Insight 2: *The trust won over a lifetime of service was washed away in a trice due to a single bad trait, that is greed.*

His greed even squashed his mental abilities as well as any moral scruples. For one thing he was unable to realise, in spite of being clever that he was giving in to criminal activity by aiding bandits in order to appease his greed. He was so blinded by his greed that he also seemed to be oblivious of the fact that he fully betrayed the total trust the villagers had in him as well as that of the King. This ruined his career and life.

If we are to be successful at any position where decision-making is significant and crucial, we must start training ourselves for it by exerting it in our own personal life : being aware of our negative character traits and making a conscious decision to work at them is a basic requisite for training ourselves for future decision-making in our careers.

18

The Bull Called Delightful

In the country of Gandhara in northern India, there was a city called Takxasila. In that city the Enlightenment Being was born as a certain calf. Since he was well-bred for strength, he was bought by a high-class rich man. He became very fond of the gentle animal, and called him 'Delightful'. He took good care of him and fed him only the best.

When Delightful grew up into a big fine strong bull, he thought, "I was brought up by this generous man. He gave me such good food and constant care, even though sometimes there were difficulties. Now I am a big grown-up bull and there is no other bull who can pull as heavy a load as I can. Therefore, I would like to use my strength to give something in return to my master."

So he said to the man, "Sir, please find some wealthy merchant who is proud of having many strong bulls. Challenge him by saying that your bull can pull one hundred heavily loaded bullock carts."

Following his advice, the high-class rich man went to such a merchant and struck up a conversation. After a while, he brought up the idea of who had the strongest bull in the city.

The merchant said, "Many have bulls, but none has any as strong as mine." The rich man said, "Sir, I have a bull who can pull one-hundred heavily loaded bullock carts." "No, friend, how can there be such a bull? That is unbelievable!" said the merchant. The other replied, "I do have such a bull, and I am willing to make a bet."

The merchant said, "I will bet a thousand gold coins that your bull cannot pull a hundred loaded bullock carts." So the bet was made and they agreed on a date and time for the challenge.

The merchant attached together one-hundred big bullock carts. He filled them with sand and gravel to make them very heavy.

The high-class rich man fed the finest rice to the bull called Delightful. He bathed him and decorated him and hung a beautiful garland of flowers around his neck. Then he harnessed him to the first cart and climbed up onto it. Being so high class, he could not resist the urge to make himself seem very important. So he cracked a whip in the air, and yelled at the faithful bull, "Pull, you dumb animal! I command you to pull, you big dummy!"

The bull called Delightful thought, "This challenge was my idea! I have never done anything bad to my master, and yet he insults me with such hard and harsh words!" So he remained in his place and refused to pull the carts.

The merchant laughed and demanded his winnings from the bet. The high-class rich man had to pay him the one-thousand gold coins. He returned home and sat down, saddened by his lost bet, and embarrassed by the blow to his pride.

The bull called Delightful grazed peacefully on his way home. When he arrived, he saw his master sadly lying on his side. He asked. "Sir, why are you lying there like that? Are you sleeping? You look sad." The man said, "I lost a thousand gold coins because of you. With such a loss, how could I sleep?"

The bull replied, "Sir, you called me 'dummy'. You even cracked a whip in the air over my head. In all my life, did I ever break anything, step on anything, make a mess in the wrong place, or behave like a 'dummy' in any way?" He answered, "No, my pet."

The bull called Delightful said, "Then sir, why did you call me 'dumb animal', and insult me even in the presence of others? The fault is yours. I have done nothing wrong. But since I feel sorry for you, go again to the merchant and make the same bet for two-thousand gold coins. And remember to use only the respectful words I deserve so well."

Then the high-class rich man went back to the merchant and made the bet for two-thousand gold coins. The merchant thought it would be easy money. Again he set up the one-hundred heavily loaded bullock carts. Again the rich man fed and bathed the bull, and hung a garland of flowers around his neck.

When all was ready, the rich man touched Delightful's forehead with a lotus blossom, having given up the whip. Thinking of him as fondly as if he were his own child, he said. "My son, please do me the honour of pulling these one-hundred bullock carts."

Lo and behold, the wonderful bull pulled with all his might and dragged the heavy carts, until the last one stood in the place of the first.

The merchant, with his mouth hanging open in disbelief, had to pay the two-thousand gold coins. The onlookers were so impressed that they honoured the bull called Delightful with gifts. But even more important to the high-class rich man than his winnings, was his valuable lesson in humility and respect.

Insight : *Genuine courtesy and politeness show that a person is well-bred and using such manners elevates one to a superior level . People with a superior moral character will be humble and polite. Those who like to make a show of their power by being rude to others only succeed in making a show of their own inferiority and lack of moral integrity.*

Harsh words cause hurt and create ill feelings and create only negativity in the environment around the speaker-- they bring no reward. Respectful words bring honour to all and sow the seeds of joy around us.

19

The Phony Holy Man

Once there was a man who looked and acted just like a holy man. He wore nothing but rags, had long matted hair, and relied on a little village to support him. But he was sneaky and tricky. He only pretended to give up attachment to the everyday world. He was a phoney holy man.

A wealthy man living in the village wanted to earn merit by doing good deeds. So he had a simple little temple built in the nearby forest for the holy man to live in. He also fed him the finest foods from his own home.

He thought this holy man with matted hair was sincere and good, one who would not do anything unwholesome. Since he was afraid of bandits, he took his family fortune of 100 gold coins to the little temple. He buried it under the ground and said to the holy man, "Venerable one, please look after this my family fortune."

The holy man replied, "There's no need to worry about such things with people like me. We holy ones have given up attachment to the ordinary world. We have no greed or desire to obtain the possessions of others."

"Very well, venerable one," said the man. He left thinking himself very wise indeed, to trust such a good holy man.

However, the wicked holy man thought, "Aha! This treasure of 100 gold coins is enough for me to live on for the rest of my life! I will never have to work or beg again!" So a few days later he dug up the gold and secretly buried it near the roadside.

The next day he went to the wealthy villager's home for lunch as usual. After eating his fill he said, "Most honourable gentleman, I have lived here supported by you for a long time. But holy ones who have given up the world are not supposed to become too attached to one village or supporter. It would make a holy man like me impure! Therefore, kindly permit me to humbly go on my way."

The man pleaded with him again and again not to go, but it was useless. "Go then, venerable sir," he agreed at last. He went with him as far as the boundary of the village and left him there.

After going on a short way himself, the phoney holy man thought, "I must make absolutely sure that the stupid villager does not suspect me. He trusts me so much that he will believe anything. So I will deceive him with a clever trick!" He stuck a blade of dry grass in his matted hair and went back.

When he saw him returning, the wealthy villager asked, "Venerable one, why have you come back?" He replied, "Dear friend, this blade of grass from the thatched roof of your house has stuck in my hair. It is most unwholesome and impure for a holy one such as myself to 'take what is not given'."

The amazed villager said, "Think nothing of it, your reverence. Please put it down and continue on your way. Venerable ones such as you do not even take a blade of grass that belongs to another. How marvellous! How exalted you are, the purest of the holy. How lucky I was to be able to support you!" More trusting than ever, he bowed respectfully and sent him on his way again.

It just so happened that the Enlightenment Being was living the life of a trader at that time. He was in the midst of a trading trip when he stopped overnight at the village. He had overheard the entire conversation between the villager and the 'purest of the holy'. He thought, "That sounds ridiculous! This man must have stolen something far more valuable than the blade of dry grass he has made such a big show of returning to its rightful owner."

The trader asked the wealthy villager, "Friend, did you perhaps give anything to this holy looking man for safekeeping?" "Yes friend," he replied, "I trusted him to guard my family fortune of 100 gold coins." "I advise you to go and see if they are where you left them," said the trader.

Suddenly worried, he ran to the forest temple, dug up the ground, and found his treasure gone. He ran back to the trader and said, "It has been stolen!" "Friend," he replied, "No one but that so-called holy man could have taken it. Let's catch him and get your treasure back."

They both chased after him as fast as they could. When they caught up with him they made him tell where he had hidden the money. They went to the hiding place by the roadside and dug up the buried treasure.

Looking at the gleaming gold the Bodhisatta said, "You hypocritical holy man. You spoke well those beautiful words, admired by all, that one is not to 'take what is not given'. You hesitated to leave with even a blade of grass that didn't belong to you. But it was so easy for you to steal a hundred gold coins!" After ridiculing the way he had acted in this way, he advised him to change his ways for his own good.

Insight: *Be careful of any man who puts on a big show of his honesty and be even more wary of a holy man who does not mind doing that. For that matter anyone who makes a big show of his good qualities is not to be taken at his word. It would be safer to investigate his claims. The actions of those who are really good speak for themselves. Those who really have good qualities and are honest show their qualities through their deeds and neither boast about it nor do they put on an exaggerated show of artificial goodness.*

20

One Way Hospitality

There were two merchants who wrote letters back and forth to each other. They never met face to face. One lived in Varanasi and the other lived in a remote border village.

The country merchant sent a large caravan to Varanasi. It had 500 carts loaded with fruits and vegetables and other products. He told his workers to trade all these goods with the help of the Varanasi merchant.

When they arrived in the big city, they went directly to the merchant. They gave him the gifts they had brought. He was pleased and invited them to stay in his own home. He even gave them money for their living expenses. He treated them with the very best hospitality. He asked about the well-being of the country merchant and gave them gifts to take back to him. Since it is easier for a local person to get a good price, he saw to it that all their goods were fairly traded. They returned home and told their master all that had happened.

Later on, the Varanasi merchant sent a caravan of 500 carts to the border village. His workers also took gifts for the country merchant. When they arrived he asked, “Where do you come from?” They said they came from the Varanasi merchant, the one who wrote him letters.

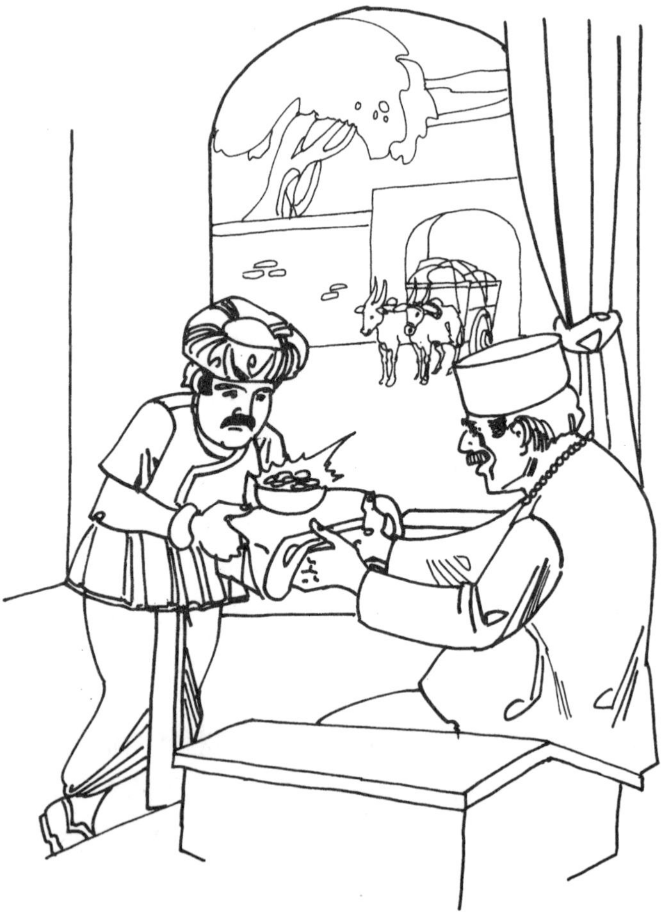

Taking the gifts, the country merchant laughed in a very discourteous way and said, “Anyone could say they came from the Varanasi merchant!” Then he sent them away, giving them no place to stay, no gifts, and no help at all.

The caravan workers went downtown to the marketplace and did their business without local help. They returned to Varanasi and told their master all that had happened.

Before too long, the country merchant sent another caravan of 500 carts to Varanasi. Again his workers took gifts to the same merchant. When his workers saw them coming, they said to him, "We know just how to provide suitable lodgings, food and expense money for these people."

They took them outside the city walls to a good place to camp for the night. They said they would return to Varanasi and prepare food and get expense money for them.

Instead they rounded up all their fellow workers and returned to the campsite in the middle of the night. They robbed all 500 carts, including the workers' outer garments. They chased away the bullocks, and removed and carried off the cart wheels.

The villagers were terrified. They ran back home as fast as their legs could carry them.

The city merchant's workers told him all they had done. He said, 'Those who forget gratitude and ignore simple hospitality wind up getting what they deserve. Those who do not appreciate the help they have received soon find that no one will help them anymore."

Insight: *If you don't help others, you can't expect them to help you.*

How many ways are there of saying the same thing?

"Do unto others as you would like it to be done to yourself."

Love thy neighbour as thy own self."

It is a commandment given by Jesus Christ.

If you want to be treated decently, first you have to treat others that way.

21

Poison Dice

There was a rich man living in Varanasi who was addicted to gambling. He played dice with another gambling addict, a man whose mind worked in tricky ways.

While the rich gambler was very honest and above board, the tricky one was dishonest. When he kept on winning he kept on playing. But when he began to lose he secretly put one of the dice in his mouth and swallowed it. Then he claimed it was lost and stopped the game.

The rich gambler began to notice this trick. Then one day he decided to teach him a lesson. He smeared poison on the dice and let it dry so it was invisible. He took these dice to the usual place and said, "Let's play dice!"

His friend agreed. They set up the gambling board and began to play. As usual the tricky one began by winning every throw of the dice. But as soon as he began to lose he sneaked the dice into his mouth.

Seeing this the rich gambler thought, "Swallow now, and then something you don't expect will happen. Your own dishonesty will make you suffer much."

After swallowing the poison dice the trickster fell down sick and fainted. The rich gambler, who was basically good at heart, thought, "Enough is enough. Now I must save his life."

He made a medical mixture to cause vomiting. He made him swallow it, and he threw up the poison dice. He gave him a drink made with clear butter, thick palm syrup, honey and cane sugar. This made the trickster feel just fine again.

Afterwards he advised him not to deceive a trusting friend again. Eventually both gamblers died and were reborn as they deserved.

Insight: *We have an innate knowledge of right and wrong and if we blatantly ignore our commonsense and silence our conscience for sheer greed, someoneelse gets a chance to take revenge or teach us a lesson. Or sometimes circumstances in our life develop in such a way that we finally learn a lesson the hard way about the results of deceit and cheating.*

Deceiving a friend may create excessive anger and animosity and so the result may be hazardous to your health and even to your life...

22

Fear Maker and Little Archer

Some say that the world comes into being, disappears, and comes into being ... over and over, throughout time. In one of these previous worlds, countless years ago, Truth was unknown and the Five Training Steps were practised by only a few. Even the Enlightenment Being - the Bodhisatta - did not know Truth, and had not yet discovered the Five Training Steps.

Once in that long ago world, there was a king named Brahmadatta. Like many other kings of that name, he ruled in the place known today as Varanasi.

The Bodhisatta was born in a rich high-class family in a market town, also in northern India. He happened to be a dwarf, bent over and partly hunchbacked. When he became a young man he remained short and stooped. Many people found him unpleasant to look at.

He studied under a very outstanding teacher. He learned all there was to know. at that time, about the two great branches of knowledge - religion and science. He also learned how to use a bow and arrow better than anyone else in India. For this reason his teacher called him 'Little Archer'.

Like most new graduates he was quite clever. He thought, "Many people judge by appearance alone. If I go to a king and ask for a job, he'll probably ask, 'Having such a short body, what can you possibly do for me?' Therefore it would be better if I can team up with a front man - someone who is handsome in appearance, tall and well-grown in body, and strong in personality. I will provide the brains, but remain out of sight behind his shadow. In this way we can earn a good living together."

One day he was walking in the district where the weavers lived and worked. He happened to see a big, strong looking man. He greeted him and asked his name. The weaver said, "Because of my appearance, people call me Fear Maker."

"With such an impressive name." said Little Archer, "and being so big and strong looking, why do you have such a low-paying job?" "Because life is hard," he replied.

"I have an idea." said the dwarf "In all India there is no one as skilled with a bow and arrow as I am. But I don't look the part! If I asked a king for work he would either laugh or get angry at me. He would not believe that a hunchbacked little dwarf could be the greatest archer in India!

'But you look perfect. And your name helps too. Therefore, let us go together to the king. You will be thc front man and do all the talking. The king will hire you immediately. Meanwhile I will remain as if hidden underneath your shadow. I will be the real archer and we will prosper and be happy. You just have to do whatever I tell you."

Thinking he had nothing to lose, Fear Maker agreed, saying, "It's a deal, my friend!"

The two partners went off to Varanasi to see the king. When they entered the throne room, they bowed respectfully to the king. He asked them, "Why have you come here?"

Fear Maker stood in front and did all the talking. He answered, "I am the great archer known as Fear Maker. There is no one in all India who understands the science of archery as well as I do. I wish to be in your service, your majesty."

The king was quite impressed. He asked, "What shall I pay you?" "I will serve you for 500 pieces of money per week, your majesty," he replied.

Nodding, the king noticed the silent dwarf stooping behind him, almost out of sight. "Who is this little man?" he asked. "What does he do for you?" "He's my little assistant," said Fear Maker. 'Very well," said King Brahmadatta, "the job is yours."

In this way Fear Maker was accepted into the king's service, but it was Little Archer who did all the work.

Before long, news came to the palace that there was a ferocious tiger living in the jungle next to the king's highway. He ambushed travellers, and then killed and ate them. Many began to avoid the king's highway out of fear of the man-eater.

The king summoned Fear Maker and asked, "Can you capture this rampaging tiger, young man?" "Your majesty," he answered, "I am known as your best archer. Why wouldn't I be able to capture a tiger?" Hearing this, the king gave him an extra sum of money and sent him out to catch the tiger.

Fear Maker went home and told all this to his partner. "All right," said Little Archer, "be on your way!" "Aren't you coming too?" asked the surprised Fear Maker. "No, I won't go," he replied, "but I will give you a perfect plan. You must do exactly as I say." "I will, my little friend. Please tell me," said the big front man.

The clever little dwarf said to his friend, "Go to the district of the tiger, but don't rush straight to his home by yourself. Instead, gather together a thousand local villagers and give them all bows and arrows. Take them directly to the tiger's home. But then you must let them go on ahead while you hide in the underbrush.

'The local villagers will be very afraid of the tiger. When they see him they will surround him and beat him. Being so terrified, they won't stop beating him until he's dead!

"Meanwhile you must cut a piece of vine with your teeth. Then come out of hiding and approach the dead tiger, holding the vine in your hand. When you see the tiger's body, shout at the people, 'Hey! Who has killed the tiger? I was going to capture him with this vine and lead him like a bull to the king. That's why I've been searching in the jungle. Now tell me who has killed the tiger before I could get here with my vine.'

"The villagers will be easily frightened by this. They will say, 'Lord Fear Maker, please don't tell the king! Then they will give you a big bribe to be quiet. Thinking you have killed the dangerous tiger, King Brahmadatta will also reward you greatly." This was the tricky plan of the clever Little Archer.

Fear Maker did exactly as he had been instructed. The man-eating tiger was killed, and fear was removed from that part of the king's highway. Followed by a big crowd he returned to the king and said, "Your majesty, I have killed the tiger and made the jungle safe for people again." The king was pleased and gave him a huge reward.

Before long there were similar complaints about a buffalo who threatened another royal road. Again the king sent Fear Maker. Following Little Archer's strategy he did exactly as before. He took credit for killing the buffalo and was greatly rewarded again by the grateful king.

By this time Fear Maker had become a very rich and powerful nobleman. All the wealth and praise, which he didn't really deserve, soon went to his head. He became intoxicated with his own conceit.

and began thinking he was a 'big man' in his own right. He even looked down on Little Archer and ignored his advice. He said to him, "You think this is all because of you. But I don't need you. I can do all this without you!" He had come to believe in the appearance created by Little Archer's plan.

Then it happened that an enemy king attacked. He surrounded the city of Varanasi with his army. He sent a message to King Brahmadatta that he must either surrender his kingdom or wage war. The King of Varanasi ordered his greatest hero, Fear Maker, to go out and fight the enemy.

Fear Maker was dressed in full military armour. He mounted the mightiest armoured war elephant. Little Archer knew that the ungrateful conceited braggart, called Fear Maker. was really scared to death underneath. So he too mounted the elephant and sat behind Fear Maker. The mighty elephant walked through the city gates towards the battlefield, followed by a big crowd.

When Fear Maker heard the huge noise made by the war drums, he began trembling with fear.To keep him from falling off the elephant and being killed, Little Archer tied a rope around him and held him with it.

When Fear Maker saw the field of battle he was overwhelmed by the terrible fear of death. So much so, that he couldn't help but release his bowels and urinate at the same time—all over the back of the poor brave war elephant!

The Enlightenment Being said, "Earlier you bragged and spoke roughly like a big man. But now, the only big thing you do is make a filthy mess all over this elephant's back! Your present actions prove your past appearance was false."

Fear Maker had embarrassed himself. Little Archer had humbled him by speaking the truth. But he couldn't help feeling sympathy for him. He said, "Don't be afraid anymore, my friend. With me to protect you, your life is safe. Climb down from the elephant and go home and take a bath."

Alone atop the great elephant, the Enlightenment Being thought, "Now is the time to show what is in the heart of this hunchbacked little dwarf!" Shouting mightily as he rode he charged into the field of battle. Without killing any men or animals, he crashed through the enemy's defences. He broke into the king's camp, captured him, and took him back as prisoner to the King of Benares.

King Brahmadatta was delighted with Little Archer's great victory. He rewarded him with wealth and fame. He became known throughout all India as 'Little Archer the Wise'. He sent his friend Fear Maker back to his home village and supported him with monthly payments.

Little Archer the Wise practised generosity and other meritorious deeds. When he died he was reborn as he deserved.

Insight: *The brains and skills of Little Archer are used to made his assistant Fear Maker look like a great and brave man and eventually Fear Maker forgot what was behind his apparent success and not only started believing that this success was solely his own but also he became so conceited that he though he did not need the support of Little Archer at all. The test came when he had to fight the enemy face to face and this brought him back to reality and gave him a real picture of his courage. It was lucky for him that Little Archer did not take the opportunity to teach him a lesson and leave him at the mercy of the enemy. True greatness is depicted by little Archer at this stage when he protected Fear Maker in spite of his having told him a while ago: "I don't need you."*

The moral is: *Our mind can play tricks on us and make us believe a great lie when we get appreciation from other people based on appearances: others think we are great and we start believing we are really so. So what we need to know in regard to the world around us is that "Appearances can be deceiving," Also, more important still, we need to apply this dictum to our own self so we can constantly have a reality check in our lives.*

23

The Careless Lion

Many years ago, the Five Training Steps were not yet known in the world. There was a very wealthy man living in Varanasi who owned a large herd of cattle. He hired a man to look after them.

During the time of year when the rice paddies were filled with the green growing rice plants, the herdsman took the cattle to the forest to graze. From there he brought the milk and butter and cheese to the rich man in Varanasi.

It just so happened that. being in the forest put the cattle in a very frightening situation. There was a meat-eating lion living nearby. Sensing the presence of the lion kept the cattle in constant fear. This made the cows tense and high-strung, leaving them too weak to give more than a little milk.

One day the owner of the cattle asked the herdsman why he was bringing such a small amount of milk and butter and cheese. He replied, "Sir, cows need to be calm and contented to give much milk. Due to a nearby lion, your cows are always afraid and tense. So they give hardly any milk."

"I see. " said the rich man. Thinking like an animal trapper, he asked, "Is the lion closely connected to any other animal?" The herdsman answered, "Sir, there happens to be a variety of deer living in the forest. They are called 'minideer' because they are very small. Even the adults only grow to be about one foot tall. The lion has become very friendly with a certain minideer doe."

The rich man of Varanasi said, "So that my cows will be at peace and able to give their usual milk, this is what you are to do. Capture the lion's friend and rub poison all over her body. Then wait a couple days before releasing her. She will be like bait in a trap for the lion. When he dies, bring his body to me. Then my cows will be safe and happy again."

The herdsman followed his boss's orders exactly. When the lion saw his favorite minideer doe, he was so overjoyed that he threw all caution to the wind. Without even sniffing the air around her, he immediately began licking her excitedly all over. Because of too much joy and not enough caution, he fell into the poisonous trap. The poor lion died on the spot.

> ***Insight:*** *As a leader and decision maker you need to be cautious about your vulnerability. Anyone who has a weak point has to be very careful either to hide it or be very careful that nobody uses it to drag you down. Since it is not easy to do either of these things, it is advisable to put in as much effort as possible to get rid of those weak points or at least tone them down as much as possible.*
>
> *Indulging in our fancies may bring some deep satisfaction but as it proved to be for the Lion in this story indulging too much in a good thing is like advertising your weakness and it can prove to be dangerous or even fatal.*

24

Clear-sighted—the Great, King of the World

It is said that there are two ways to practise religion. One is to live apart from the ordinary everyday world as a monk, a nun or a holy one. Those who are sincere in this way have as their highest goal the direct experience of complete Truth - full Enlightenment.

The other way to practise religion is within the ordinary world. Those who are sincere in this way have as their highest goal the harmony of an undivided world, living peacefully under a perfectly wholesome ruler—a 'King of the World'.

Once the Enlightenment Being was born and given the name 'Clear-sighted'. As he grew up he developed ten rules of good government:

- absence of hidden ill will;
- absence of open hostility,
- harmlessness,
- self-control,

- patience,
- gentleness,
- charity,
- generosity,
- straightforwardness and
- goodness.

The people of the world began to notice the wholesomeness and fairness of Clear-sighted, who lived strictly according to these rules. Gradually, those in his vicinity volunteered to live under his authority as king, rather than under the dishonest politicians of the time.

As his reputation spread, every king in the world came to Clear-sighted and said, "Come, oh lord. You are welcome. My kingdom is your kingdom. Advise me how to rule in your name."

Then Clear-sighted said,

- "Do not destroy life.
- Do not take what is not given.
- Do not behave wrongly in sexual matters.
- Do not speak falsely.
- Do not take alcohol that clouds the mind."

He continued, "My commands to the world are only these five. As long as these five are obeyed, my sixth rule is freedom for all to follow local customs and religions."

After all the people on earth had come to live under his peaceful rule, he became known as Clear-sighted, the Great, King of the World. His royal city, the capital of the whole world, was called Kusavati. It was a beautiful and prosperous city with four magnificent gates—one golden, one silver, one jade and one crystal.

Outside the gates, Kusavati was surrounded by seven rows of palm trees—a row with golden trunks and silver leaves and fruits; a row with silver trunks and golden leaves and fruits; a row with cat's-eye trunks and crystal leaves and fruits; a row with crystal trunks and cat's-eye leaves and fruits; a row with agate trunks and coral leaves and fruits; a row with coral trunks and agate leaves and fruits; and finally a row with trunks and leaves and fruits of every kind of jewel found in the world!

When breeze blew through these marvelous palms, the sweet sounds of gentle music were heard throughout the city. This music was so enticing and pleasant that some of the citizens were enchanted into stopping their work and dancing for joy!

Clear-sighted, the Great, King of the World, had a couch encrusted with jewels from the wonderful palms. After a long, righteous and peaceful reign, he lay on the rich couch for the last time. He knew that his end was near.

Of all his 84 queens, the one who loved him most was called, 'Most-pleasant'. Sensing the state of his mind she said, "You rule over all the cities of the world, including this beautiful Kusavati with its four magnificent gates and seven rows of marvelous palms. Think about this and be happy!"

The King of the World said, "No, my dear queen. don't say that. Instead you should advise me to give up attachment to the cities of the world and all they contain." Surprised. she asked, "Why do you say this, my lord?" "Because today I will die," he said.

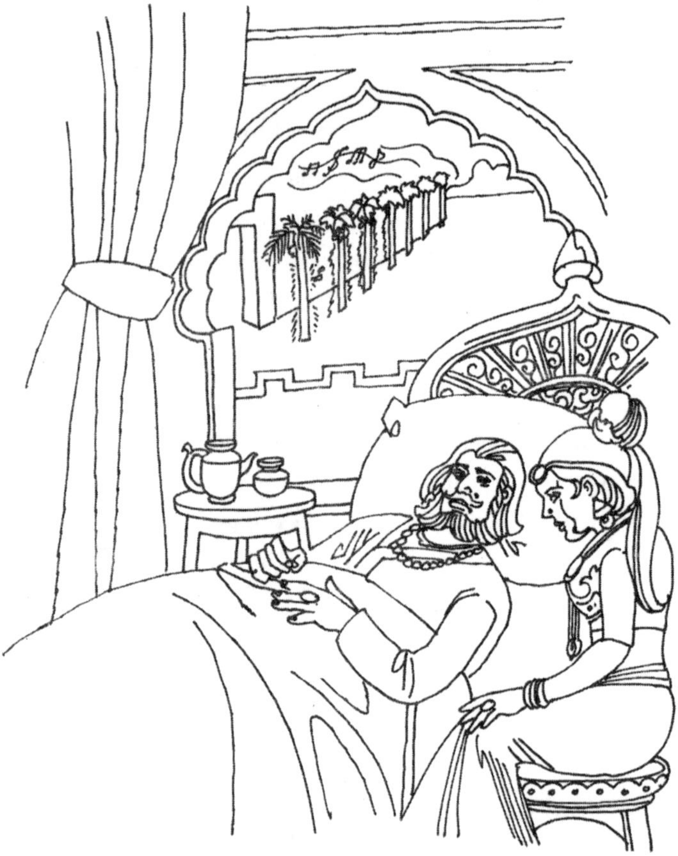

Then Queen Most-pleasant started to cry, wiping away the tears as they flowed. And all the other queens also broke into tears. And the king's ministers and his whole court, both men and women, could not keep from weeping and sobbing. All eyes overflowed with tears.

But King Clear-sighted, the Great said, "Your tears are useless. Be at peace." Hearing this the wailing subsided and his subjects were silent.

Then he said to Queen Most-pleasant, "Oh my queen, do not cry, do not lament. Anything that comes into being, whether it be a kingdom including the whole world, or just a tiny sesame seed—it cannot last forever. Anyone who is born, whether it be the King of the World, or the poorest petty thief—all must decay and die. Whatever is built up, falls apart. Whatever is born or is created by us, decays. The only true happiness is in the moment when living beings and things come into being and are far from death and decay."

In this way the Enlightenment Being got them to think about what most people don't want to think about—that all things come to an end. He advised them to be generous and wholesome. Then the King of the World, like everyone else, died.

Insight: *This story is the best lesson one has heard of, about accepting our impermanence and the hard reality that however good life may be for some people yet it has to come to a end, without exception. So also all other things too have to come to an end and there are no two ways about this fact.*

Also the other side of the coin is shown to us with subtlety : the level-headed king who knew and accepted his impermanence gave his life to building a heaven, right here on earth. And the unspoken question is "What can we do with our lives to make the earth a better place?"

Besides the King did not waste a moment wailing like his subjects, even when he knew that his end was near but rather he helped his courtiers accept the end that was inevitable So a heavenly place was created for his subjects as the king. constantly had a thought for those around him, till the end...

Conclusion:
Ten Keys to Enlightened Decision-making

Decisions are about choices which are determined by the values we uphold. The stories in the Jataka and their insight provide the values necessary for enlightened decision-making. They can be summarised in the cultivation of the following Ten Perfections:

- energy,
- determination,
- truthfulness,
- wholesomeness,
- detachment,
- evenmindedness,
- wisdom,
- patience,
- generosity, and
- loving-kindness.

Even with the right values no one makes the right decision every time. But by developing your decision-making routine, you can increase your success rate!

Anatomy of a Decision

Making a good decision requires patience and careful thought. Following a step-by-step approach can help.

Step 1: Define the problem.

Size up the situation.

- Examine the problem thoroughly—look at it from all angles.
- Keep thinking—don't be satisfied with quick, easy answers.
- Avoid mistaking the problem's symptoms (for example, a shortage of money) for the problem itself (poor spending habits, too much debt, etc.).

Set goals and priorities. Ask yourself:

- "What do I want to achieve by making this decision—what are my goals?"
- "Which of these goals must I meet in order to solve this problem—what are my priorities?" Write down your goals and priorities and review them often.

Try to put your goals in measurable terms (time, money, etc.) so you can measure your success later on.

Step 2: Re-evaluate the situation. (step 1 may have changed your view of the problem!)

Consider your options. Once you've identified the problem, ask yourself:

- "Do I need to take action in order to achieve my goals and priorities?"
- "Will this problem solve itself with time?"

Don't make unnecessary decisions. Beware that the best decision may be to do nothing for the time being. But don't delay just to avoid making a tough or unpleasant decision. Be honest with yourself! If you decide that action is needed, proceed to step 3.

Step 3: Gather information. In order to solve a problem, you should make yourself an 'expert' on the subject.

Use your time wisely. If a decision is not immediately necessary, use your time to gather information. (Be sure you leave enough time to act on your decision, though.)

Seek advice. Get help from people who know more about the details of the problem. Don't be afraid to admit that you don't know something.

Use all resources. Use the library, employee records and any source of facts on the problem.

Step 4: Think of alternatives. At this stage of the decision-making process, any idea is a good idea.

Be open. Don't limit yourself to ideas that sound 'reasonable.' Try 'brainstorming' (listing anything and everything that comes to mind).

Don't judge. Avoid jumping to conclusions. Gather all your ideas before considering your alternatives.

Record your ideas. Put all your thoughts on paper, so you can evaluate them later.

Step 5: Choose an alternative. Test each alternative carefully to see how it measures up against the others.

Think ahead. Try to imagine the consequences of each alternative. Ask yourself, "What will happen if...?" Be thorough, and give each plan a chance.

Be practical. Make sure your plans can be carried out. For example, does your organisation have the equipment to make the changes you have in mind? Is the solution more expensive than the problem?

Be creative. If necessary, combine the best features of several different ideas. Make a new alternative—one that works!

Choose the alternative that will best achieve the goals and priorities you identified in Step 1.

Step 6: Put your decision to work

Take action. Don't satisfy yourself with simply having made a tough decision. A good decision means nothing until it's put into effect.

Inform others. Make sure everyone affected by your decision knows what will change, and why. Explain what improvements they can expect as a result of your decision. Ask for feedback.

Follow up on your plan. Check from time to time to see that any changes you made are still in effect—or to see if adjustments are needed. Also, make sure the problem you solved has not returned or taken another form.

The 'Art' and 'Science' of Making a Decision

Your intuition and your analytical skills can both be helpful—if you know how to put them to work for you.

Intuition is the ability to know or feel something without using logic or reason. Your intuition can help you:

- Create Ideas, providing a starting point for further thought.
- Solve "Why?" Or "Should I?" Problems - when the answer may be based on feelings, values or opinions.
- Break a deadlock in your mind between different solutions.

Analytical skill is the ability to use logic to examine and measure a problem. Your analytical skills can help you:

- Examine the ideas generated by your intuition, to separate the workable ideas from the worthless.
- Solve "How To" Or "How Many" problems -when the choices can be tested in terms of cold, hard fact (for example, "Is this technique more efficient?" or "Do I have time for both activities?").